Werner Cohn

with a foreword by
Edward Alexander

Avukah Press
Cambridge, MA

Avukah Press
Cambridge, MA

Library of Congress Cataloging-in-Publication Data

Cohn, Werner 1926-
Partners in Hate: Noam Chomsky and the Holocaust
Deniers
Werner Cohn; with a foreword by Edward Alexander
p. 186
Includes index

ISBN 0-964-58970-2

1. Holocaust, Jewish (1939-1945) — Errors,
inventions, etc.
2. Holocaust, Jewish (1939) – Historiography

Contents

PUBLISHER'S NOTE   i

FOREWORD by Edward Alexander   1

PREFACE   13

THE HIDDEN ALLIANCES OF
NOAM CHOMSKY   37

REFERENCES CITED   153

INDEX   161

Publisher's Note

Avukah Press is proud to announce as its first published work *Partners in Hate: Noam Chomsky and the Holocaust Deniers*, Werner Cohn's revelatory work chronicling the activist MIT professor's relationship to neo-Nazi Holocaust deniers on two continents.

Some readers may be familiar with *The Hidden Alliances of Noam Chomsky*, the essay that makes up the body of this book, which was first published by Americans for a Safe Israel (AFSI) in 1988 and included in *With Friends Like These: The Jewish Critics of Israel* (SPI Books) edited by Edward Alexander, in 1993. *Partners in Hate* represents the first publication of Cohn's essay in its entirety, with a new introduction by the author as well as commentary from Edward Alexander.

Some writers who have noted Noam Chomsky's relationships with the denial movement have chosen to dismiss them as "antics" or just one more manifestation of the linguist-turned-activist's political eccentricities. Cohn, in contrast, illuminates the significance of the Chomsky-Faurisson Affair, chronicling the details of the Chomsky-Faurisson relationship, tracing the peculiar origins of the Nazi apologists lingering at the fringe of far-left French politics, and tying it all together with a piercing analysis of some of Chomsky's more familiar anti-

Israel polemics — work the deniers themselves hail as dovetailing with their own mission to demonize Jews. This multi-tiered analysis should give pause to those who continue to uphold Chomsky's version of these events with the standard invocation of Voltairian free-speech arguments or the fraying "anti-Zionist but not antisemitic" defense.

Of course, the significance of the Chomsky-Faurisson affair goes far beyond the activities of a few radicals who have crossed the line into hate trafficking. While the Jews seem to have survived this brutal century, so too has antisemitism which is ready to march into the next millennium wrapped in both the humanistic, universalistic vocabulary of the Left as well as the racist language of the Right. As Cohn points out in his introduction, this is "the true significance of the Chomsky phenomenon," a reprieve for the oldest hatred for which Chomsky and other like-minded thinkers must bear some responsibility.

Since the *Hidden Alliances* story first came to light, many of the characters in the Chomsky tale have fallen on hard times. While Chomsky himself continues to publish books at a rate which would dazzle the most prolific writers of pulp-fiction (an impressive feat for a man whom supporters claim is "covertly banned" in the U.S.), *La Vieille Taupe*, French publisher of the Holocaust-denial literature of Robert Faurisson, is today little more than the home address of its founder, Robert Guillaume. *Ogmios*, the Paris-based, right-wing bookstore-cum-movement (joint publishers with *La Vieille Taupe* of a

Holocaust-denial periodical), has closed and reopened as *La Librarie* .

While Faurisson himself is a regular contributor to the Institute for Historical Review (IHR), the American branch of the Holocaust denial movement, the IHR itself has been facing financial difficulties with the departure of the organization's wealthy benefactor Willis Carto. (Carto, financier of numerous right-wing groups, has declared war on his former allies in the IHR through his rival organization the Liberty Lobby.) As a result of this conflict, publication of Faurisson's *Memoire en Défense*, the book in which "The Chomsky Preface" first appeared, scheduled for publication in November 1994 has been postponed indefinitely.

Publisher's Note

One hopes that the light of reason, exemplified by the work of Cohn, Alexander and others, illuminating these groups and their hate-filled ideas, will help speed their demise.

Avukah Press hopes to continue to shine the light of reason by publishing books that examine how various parts of the political spectrum have dealt with issues of Jews, Zionism and antisemitism.

Avukah, literally "torch," was a Zionist student organization which existed on U.S. college campuses from 1925 to 1943. In those two event-filled decades, Avukah grappled with all of the issues that still affect American and world Jewry today: Jewish identity, nation building, religious, spiritual and political renewal, with tough-minded dedication. Their methods, education, discussion and vigorous debate,

Publisher's Note

can be seen in their literature which can be found on the shelves of many Jewish libraries.

It is with great pride and an understanding of the responsibility associated with reawakening the Avukah name that Avukah Press introduces the first of its titles.

Jon Haber   **Hillel Stavis**

Foreword

Edward Alexander

It is a commonplace of modern history that extremes of left and right often meet, as when Nazi Foreign Minister Ribbentrop in 1939 flew to Moscow to join Stalin in the non-aggression pact that prepared the invasion of Poland. Many extreme leftists have become violent rightists, and many Nazis have turned Communist. Noam Chomsky's singular distinction as a political activist is a perverse eclecticism that unites the worst of both extremes. He may be the only writer published and trumpeted by the leftist *Nation* and the neo-Nazi *Journal of Historical Review*, which, as Werner Cohn points out, promotes his books and tapes on Israel along with the works of Josef Goebbels as the authoritative word on the subject of the nefarious Jews. The dead water, the point of pause, of the opposite eddies of pollution unleashed by communism and Nazism is the brain of Noam Chomsky.

We are indebted to Werner Cohn for his diligence and tenacity in exploring and then analyzing Chomsky's elaborate ties to the neo-Nazi Holocaust deniers in France and elsewhere. To wade through the quaint and curious lucubrations of such polemicists as Robert Faurisson and Pierre Guillaume, to say nothing of Chomsky himself, requires the intellectual equivalent of hip-boots. Given the unfamiliarity of most Americans with French intellectual life, and especially with its obscure subterranean depths, Cohn's success in hunting down the facts and naming villains will enable readers of this study to see that Chomsky's "defense" of Faurisson was far more than an instance of overzealous and uncritical civil libertarianism.

Foreword

In this new edition of his study on Chomsky, Professor Cohn calls our attention to Chomsky's endorsement of a book by Israel Shahak, a Jewish (and Israeli) antisemite who has devoted himself to depicting the Talmud as the generative source of the evil that the Jews have visited (and through Zionism continue to visit) upon mankind. This is a valuable reminder that Chomsky's campaign against Israel and on behalf of the neo-Nazi "revisionists" is a modern continuation of a pathology that goes back to at least the thirteenth century, and which has come to be known as "Jewish self-hatred," a term interchangeable with Jewish antisemitism. Before Pope Gregory IX ordered the Talmud to be seized, examined, and publicly burnt in Paris and Rome, he was presented in 1239 with a detailed analysis of the manifold evils of the Jews' religious books from the Dominican brother Nicholas Donin, a Jewish convert possessed of the "special" knowledge of these poisonous books that only a Jew could have. Six centuries later Socialist antisemites heard from the converted Jew Karl Marx the allegation that capitalism is nothing other than the Talmud written in the "real" language of the Jews, which is neither Hebrew nor Yiddish, but "haggling." Jews like Marx and Shahak and Chomsky have always found it easier to join those who sought to discredit the Jewish people than to come to their defense.

I wish I could share Professor Cohn's kindly hope that old age will mellow Chomsky and make him less deserving of the prominent place he holds in the long history of Jewish self-hatred. But it seems to me that the passage of time has done nothing to diminish those qualities of mind and character, that unique blend of propagandist's tricks and low cunning, which led Arthur Schlesinger, in the December 1969 issue of *Commentary*, to label Noam Chomsky (who had been forced to confess faking "quotations" from Harry Truman) "an intellectual crook." In a 1982 review of Chomsky's book *Towards a New Cold War*, Walter Laqueur remarked that "on the rare occasions when Mr. Chomsky is dealing with facts and not with fantasies, he exaggerates by a factor of, plus or minus, four or five." Laqueur went on to describe the book as "a squalid tract, a clumsy piece of propaganda, ... a ludicrous fabrication, intellectually worthless and morally grotesque, a parody of scholarship that reminds me of the worst excesses of Hitlerism and Stalinism."

As evidence of Chomsky's dogged attachment to his ingrained hatreds and sordid methods, I offer in illustration Chomsky's recent attack on me as "'the most highly publicized' apologist for Nazi crimes." (The quotation within the quotation is a typical Chomsky fabrication.) Chomsky had been irked by references in my review (*Commentary*, November 1993) of Deborah Lipstadt's book *Denying the Holocaust* to the subject of his lengthy collaboration with Robert Faurisson and other neo-Nazis, and so decided to (as he thought) turn the tables on his critics by alleging (*Commentary*, February 1994) that I had been conducting a campaign to deny the "Holocaust" perpetrated against Gypsies and, for good measure, to obliterate the history of the suffering of American Indians and black slaves. A brief description of his technique is revealing.

The mind of the propagandist is very much like the spider in Swift's fable, "which by a lazy contemplation of four inches round, by an overweening pride, feeding and engendering on itself, turns all into excrement and venom, producing nothing at all but flyband and cobweb." Those who are morbidly curious about how Chomsky weaves his cobweb may wish to contemplate the following. In the May/June 1990 issue of *Congress Monthly* I referred, in the midst of a literary review and with no further elaboration, to "every exploded fiction about the Holocaust — ranging from the notion that not only the Jews but also Poles, Gypsies, Communists and homosexuals were chosen by the Nazis for annihilation." Here, thought Chomsky, was solid meat and drink to batten on at last — the opportunity to project one's own intentions upon the enemy and to claim, as he has done repeatedly since then (especially on the electronic mail networks) that I am the author of "pro-Nazi apologetics." For the benefit of readers who may find Chomsky's oracular intuitions here a bit murky, I will volunteer my services as logician-in-ordinary to the sage of MIT, who appears to be saying this: "You people who claim that the Jews alone were singled out by the Nazis for total destruction are the true Nazi apologists because a genuine anti-Nazi would insist [erroneously, of course] that Hitler planned to annihilate all identifiable groups except ethnic Germans." There is a kind of logic here, but it is the sort that Pierre Vidal-Naquet imputes to Chomsky in his book *Assassins of Memory*: "When logic has no other end than self-defense, it goes mad."

Chomsky, of course, does not value truth for its own sake, but has now become a champion of the Gypsies in order, so he thinks, (to) *epater les Juifs* by making Hitler into an equal-opportunity destroyer. Neither in the essay mentioned above nor anywhere else have I denied Nazi persecution, sometimes extending to murder, of Gypsies (as well as Poles and homosexuals). In the case of the Gypsies (Romani), the word "genocide," in the sense defined by Raphael Lemkin in 1943 — humiliation, dehumanization, forcible, even murderous denationalization of a group — may be appropriate. Nazi policies toward the Gypsies were unclear and inconsistent. In Germany itself the Nazis murdered the so-called "mixed" or "impure" Gypsies ("pure" Gypsies being thought of as an originally Aryan racial group); in the rest of Europe the Nazis murdered wandering Gypsy bands, but generally left sedentary Gypsies unscathed. Since some Gypsy tribes were protected, since individual Gypsies living among the rest of the population were not hunted down, since Himmler's order of November 15, 1943 stipulated that "sedentary Gypsies and part-Gypsies are to be treated as citizens of the country," and since many Gypsies served, albeit in the most dangerous assignments, in the Wehrmacht, most scholars have distinguished between the Nazi campaign against the

Gypsies and the Holocaust, the campaign to murder every single Jewish person. The scholarly journal published by Oxford University Press — *Holocaust and Genocide Studies* — recognized this distinction in its title. But distinctions are not the business of propagandists like Noam Chomsky. For him everything must be reduced to pellets of ideology small enough to be ingested by — if I may be allowed to change the metaphor I used above — a discursive mouse.

What drove Chomsky to lend his support to the neo-Nazi deniers of the Holocaust? At times he has given the impression that immaculate agnosticism moves him to defend the deniers. In *Liberation* (December 23, 1980) he wrote that "I don't know enough about [Faurisson's] work to determine if what he is claiming is accurate or not." In *Le Matin* (January 19, 1981) the newly tolerant linguist wrote that "we don't want people to have religious or dogmatic beliefs about the existence of the Holocaust." But we may conjecture that even though he does not directly endorse the claims of Faurisson and the other cranks, he wishes them well on their endeavor; for he believes that to undermine belief in the Holocaust is to undermine belief in the legitimacy of the State of Israel, which many people supposed (albeit mistakenly) to have come into existence because of Western bad conscience over what was done to the Jews of World War II. Chomsky therefore feels no compunction about joining "right-wing" forces to achieve the great desideratum of delegitimizing the Jewish state. This is one reason (among many) why such a right-wing antisemite as Joseph Sobran fondly refers to Chomsky as "a true Israelite, in whom there is no guile."

Chomsky's pretense of defending Robert Faurisson's civil liberties (free speech and academic freedom) is, of course, a fraud. Faurisson's right to teach was not withdrawn, neither was he, as the petition Chomsky promoted falsely claimed, denied access to public libraries and archives. The only important sense in which Chomsky's involvement with the Nazis concerns free speech is that, as everyone knows, Chomsky has a nasty habit of labeling all who disagree with him as enemies of freedom. Vidal-Naquet suggests in his book that Chomsky's zeal on behalf of Faurisson is unlikely to cool until the French republic passes a law requiring that Faurisson's works be read in public schools and advertised and sold at the entrances to synagogues.

Although Lipstadt assigns considerable blame to Chomsky's "Voltairean" defense of the Nazis' free speech for their ability to penetrate the campuses, she pays insufficient attention to its still darker implications. These were succinctly hinted at by the French writer Nadine Fresco when she commented on the pregnancy of the fact that Chomsy selects as his model Voltaire, the Enlightenment bigot who in 1745 said of the Jews: "You will not find in them anything but an ignorant and barbarous people who have for a long time combined the most sordid avarice with the most detestable superstition," and then added the paradoxical code: "One should not, however, burn them."

It is the singular virtue of Werner Cohn's study that he has fully and courageously explored Chomsky's version of Voltaire's pretended desire that the Jews should avoid the terrible fate that he himself has worked so hard to visit upon them.

Edward Alexander

University of Washington, Seattle

Preface

Avram Noam Chomsky, a famous linguist at the Massachusetts Institute of Technology, is known for his left-wing politics. It is the gravamen of this book, however, that these politics derive as much from the extreme right wing — particularly right-wing antisemitism — as from the rhetoric of the American Left.

• • •

In March of 1989, not long after the appearance of the first edition of this book, A. M. Rosenthal of the *New York Times* wrote a column to mark the tenth anniversary of the Israeli-Egyptian peace treaty. The column was generally favorable to Israel, although he also chided Israel for what he called its "historical error — the refusal to recognize the reality of the Palestinian people and passion."

One of Rosenthal's points was that Jordan is a Palestinian state (Jordan's territory is situated in the original British mandate of Palestine), and Rosenthal opposed the creation of a second Palestinian state in this territory. This was enough to once again provoke Noam Chomsky's legendary bile. He wrote:

> We might ask how the *Times* would react to an Arab claim that the Jews do not merit a 'second homeland' because they already have New York, with a huge Jewish population, Jewish-run media, a Jewish mayor, and domination of cultural and economic life.[1]

As it happened, Rosenthal did not use either the words or the concept of a "second homeland."

Nonetheless, Chomsky saw fit to put these words between quotation marks to attribute them to Rosenthal. Chomsky habitually, as we shall see in the body of this book, misrepresents the writings of others. But let that pass for the moment.

What is actually most noteworthy in this passage is Chomsky's unpleasant tone about the Jews of New York and the fact that his malice does not conform to familiar "anti-Zionist" left-wing doctrines. Chomsky's target here is very simply Jews, without any pretense whatever about being "anti-Zionist-but-not-antisemitic."

When Chomsky wrote these words, there was indeed a Jewish mayor in New York, and a large Jewish population. There were Jews in the media on all levels. There were also many Jews in cultural and economic pursuits in New York. These facts are not in dispute.

But what are "Jewish-run media?" What is meant by a Jewish "domination of cultural and economic life?" These hateful expressions are staples of traditional antisemitism. They suggest that Jews do not act as individuals but only as agents of a larger Jewish cabal. The antisemitic propagandist says that Jewish artists and business men and journalists do not pursue such professions as other men would. No, to him such Jewish men and women are "running" the media, "dominating" culture and the economy, all in their capacity as Jews, all for the sake of a Jewish design.

But wait a minute. Is it Chomsky himself who makes these antisemitic allegations? Or is it some unnamed antisemitic Arab? Chomsky does not say. Nor is he explicit, assuming that it isn't he but rather his hypothetical Arab who is speaking, in telling us whether he would regard the accusations as justified.

But what he fails to do explicitly he does by indirection. By mixing legitimate facts with allegations of "running" media and "dominating" culture, all in the same sentence and in the same tone, he endorses and justifies the antisemitic assertions. And he does all this without taking direct responsibility. Chomsky, as always, is — what is the word — clever.

Actually we have here a fine example of the well-known Chomskyan method of devious ambiguity. He says the antisemitic thing by very clear implication, and then, with the wink of complicity to his neo-Nazi following that we shall encounter again, there is a built-in explanation of it all to his left-wing following: it is not I who would ever say such a thing, not I at all, but how can I help it if an oppressed Arab makes such interesting observations?

•••

Hidden from tourists and from most of its citizens, the fringes of Israeli society harbor a fair number of babblers, seers, zealots, and other assorted know-alls. Such people are of interest mainly to social scientists and journalists who make a living describing the quaint and the curious. Ordinary

Israelis merely shrug a shoulder: surely Jews, like everyone else, are entitled to a quota of maniacs.

But even in Israel, tolerant as it is of the eccentric and the deranged, the case of Israel Shahak gives pause. Without a question, he is the world's most conspicuous Jewish antisemite. His specialty, moreover, is quite rare these days even among non-Jewish antisemites; quite rare, that is, since the demise of the Nazis. Like the Nazis before him, Shahak specializes in defaming the Talmud. In fact, he has made it his life's work to popularize the anti-Talmud ruminations of the 18th century German antisemite, Johann Eisenmenger.[2]

Now a retired chemist, Shahak travels the world to propound a simple thesis: Jews (with only a rare exception — guess who that might be) are evil. The Talmud teaches them to be criminal, and Zionism compounds the evil. Naturally, Shahak is an active, enthusiastic supporter of the most militant Arab terrorists.

Shahak's most recent tract, *Jewish History, Jewish Religion* (London and Boulder, Colorado, 1994) demands that Jews repent of their own sins and of the sins of their forefathers. First of all, says Shahak, Jews should now applaud, retroactively, the "popular anti-Jewish manifestations of the past," for instance the Chmielnicki massacres of 17th century Ukraine. These were "progressive" uprisings, according to Shahak.

Concerning the Jews of our day, Shahak reveals that "Jewish children are actually taught" to utter a ritual curse when passing a non-Jewish cemetery. Moreover, he tells us, "both before and after a meal, a pious Jew ritually washes his hands....On one of these two occasions he is worshipping God... but on the other he is worshipping Satan."

On its own, being so hopelessly crackpot, *Jewish History, Jewish Religion* would hardly find enough buyers to pay for its printing. But this little booklet is not on its own. It has a foreword by a famous writer, Gore Vidal, who tells us that he, Vidal, is not himself an antisemite. And it carries an enthusiastic endorsement, right on its cover, by Noam Chomsky. Says Chomsky: "Shahak is an outstanding scholar, with remarkable insight and depth of knowledge. His work is informed and penetrating, a contribution of great value."[3]

So that is how scholarship is judged these days at the Massachusetts Institute of Technology.

•••

Since the present book first appeared in 1988, there have been a number of other works, on Holocaust-denial and related subjects, that have been critical of Chomsky. But on the whole I have not found these discussions fully satisfactory. These authors have mentioned some of the more conspicuous examples of Chomsky's outrageous behavior without coming to grips with what I would regard as the underlying problem of the Chomsky phenomenon.

As this book will document in detail, Chomsky gave his name in support of Robert Faurisson, the well-known French neo-Nazi Holocaust denier. He has published in the neo-Nazi's journal. He went out of his way to have his books published by French neo-Nazis. He has promoted the antisemitic idea that the Jewish religion is basically anti-social. Nevertheless, the tenor of Chomsky criticism, as that of Chomsky admiration, has been to stress the image of Chomsky as a partisan of the political Left. Chomsky's use of antisemitic rhetoric — often not at all veiled by "anti-Zionism" — has by and large been ignored by his critics and sympathizers alike. (His handful of fully initiated followers, of course, are another matter).

How can we account for this negligence?

First, there is Chomsky's well-known deviousness, which we observed in his commentary on Rosenthal's writing. But that alone could hardly have misled the knowledgeable and sophisticated authors who have written about him (although it may indeed have played a part in certain instances).

Second there is the obscurity of much of the Chomsky publication enterprise. Some of his most malicious pronouncements have been reported in very small ultra-leftist and neo-Nazi publications, and often in French, thus remaining hidden from the general American reader.[4] The single most revealing description of his intimate involvement with the neo-Nazis was written in French by Chomsky's neo-Nazi associate, Pierre Guillaume, and was published by a very obscure neo-Nazi publisher in Paris. (I report on this essay in some detail — on pages 52-62 — and I ask the reader to pay particular attention to it). But, on the other hand, Chomsky has also made blatantly antisemitic statements, for instance his talk of "genocidal" teachings in the Jewish religion, in *The Fateful Triangle*, an accessible and widely-reviewed book.

In other words, Chomsky's famous ability to obfuscate and the obscurity of most of his publications can only partially explain why his neo-Nazi involvements have escaped wide-spread criticism.

In my view there has been a more fundamental obstacle to an understanding of the Chomsky phenomenon. I think that there is a persisting state of mind that divides the political world into "left" versus "right" and sees the "Left" as essentially incapable of primitive Jew-baiting. Even sophisticated writers can occasionally fall into this trap.

All informed people, of course, know that there has been an antisemitism of the Left. Recently often disguised as "anti-Zionism," left antisemitism has a history that goes back well into the nineteenth century.[5] Most recently it was propagated by the Soviet Union as long as it existed, by the splinter grouplets of the Left, and, not least, by the political propaganda of left-liberal Protestant Christianity.[6] But the rhetorical style has typically been different from the antisemitism of the Right. Where the latter was generally couched in racist or religious terms, identifying itself with chauvinist and xenophobic prejudices, the Left tended to use a Marxist, left-wing, humanistic vocabulary.

This difference in rhetoric has led to the false assumption that Left and Right are ideologically and socially incompatible, and that the two antisemitisms — the left and the right — similarly preclude one another. Consequently it is mistakenly taken for granted that a proponent of left-wing ideas cannot possibly be involved with old-fashioned Jew-baiting. Chomsky's most characteristic stance — that of the left-wing gladiator battling "Zionism" — turned out to be a very effective cover for him.

• • •

Benito Mussolini began his political life as a left-wing revolutionary socialist. When he founded Fascism, he abandoned neither the methods nor the doctrines of his early anti-"bourgeois" resentments.

Similarly, Hitler's revolution, "national socialism" in its self-description, used the methods, ideology, and personnel of left-wing radicals. In many parts of prewar Europe, individual Communists, Nazis, and anarchists, brawling with one another in the streets like Crips and Bloods,[7] nevertheless found it easy to move from one camp to the other as occasion demanded.[8]

The basic common ground of this Left-cum-Right, ultra-radical demimonde consisted of antisemitism, the worship of violence, and unrestrained mendacity, in short, a rejection of bourgeois respectability. These elements have fashioned a certain milieu that has persisted to our day.

Today's sects that openly declare themselves both Nazi and left wing — the "National Bolsheviks" of Europe, for instance, or the Third Position people in France and Italy —remain obscure and hidden from readers of the mainstream press.[9] Such obscurity has also enveloped *La Vieille Taupe* (to be described in this book), Chomsky's main transmission belt to the neo-Nazis. But while this milieu has often been concealed, especially in the post-war years, it occasionally does emerge and then gains public attention. When it does, it is virulent, much like the cholera. We think for a time that we have conquered it when we don't see it; but the vibrio persists hidden, ready to cause an epidemic when circumstances allow.

After the Six Day War of 1967 the Soviet Union broke diplomatic relations with Israel and the international Communist movement embarked on a bitter propaganda campaign against the Jewish state. In the course of this Communist crusade, the line between anti-Zionism and antisemitism was deliberately blurred. Anti-Stalinist Communists like the Trotskyists went further. Eager to outbid the Moscow-dominated movement, they began to use antisemitic language heretofore restricted to the radical Right: the Jews of Israel (not just the "capitalists" among them) were now an "oppressor nation;" Jews worldwide were depicted as a caste of "usurers." [10] (As we shall see, it was the anti-Stalinist extreme Left from whom Chomsky first learned his politics.)

But such fringe movements are hardly noticed by the public. It took certain notorious individuals to obtain substantial publicity, and this despite the generally fanciful, outrageous, and ridiculous nature of their public statements. These people were able to exploit a prominence or notoriety that came to them fortuitously. There are a number of such individuals, but, not counting Chomsky himself, the best known might well be Jacques Vergès.

Vergès is a French lawyer of mixed French-Vietnamese parentage, a former member of the Communist Party, later active in the New Left. He came to worldwide attention about ten years ago when he acted as defense lawyer for Klaus Barbie, a Nazi official in Lyon during the Occupation who was eventually convicted, in Lyon, of multiple murder. [11] Marcel Ophuls' remarkable documentary *Hotel*

Terminus, provides more than a few revealing insights into Maître Vergès' character and activities.

Vergès, like Chomsky, is still counted as a prominent man of the Left. He is active in the worldwide movement against the United States and Western democracies. He agitated against the French war in Algeria. He is vehemently on the side of Arab terrorists, both as defense lawyer and propagandist. At the same time he is also active in the network of Nazi recalcitrants and the neo-Nazi movement. According to Erna Paris, author of the book *Unhealed Wounds*, Vergès was initiated into the Nazi network by François Genoud, a Swiss Nazi financier whose resources apparently derive from Jewish money that was stolen during the war by the Nazis. It is Genoud's funds that probably financed the Barbie defense, as well as various Arab terrorist groups. Paris says that Genoud "personifies a hybrid of ultra-Left and neo-Nazi extremism .... One might even say he created the type."[12]

Vergès conducted Barbie's defense by staging a combination of street theater and burlesque. He asserted that the true war criminals were not the Nazis during the Second World War; no, the true criminals are the Jews, the Jews both during the war and now as Zionists, and also the French Resistance during the war. Furthermore, the government of France is guilty because of its Algerian war and similar offenses. For such reasons, said Vergès, Barbie should be acquitted. The Lyon court disagreed, to be sure, but not before Vergès had gained worldwide publicity for himself and for his ideology of the absurd.

In the summer of 1994, Vergès was once more in the news. Once again his striking, exotic face, familiar to us from the movie *Hotel Terminus*, seems to mock us with its characteristic superior smile. This time Maître Vergès represents the famous "Carlos" (Ilich Ramirez Sánchez), accused in Paris of numerous murders on behalf of Arab terrorist groups. But now there are also reports of East

German government records that implicate Vergès himself as a member of terrorist organizations.[13]

Vergès and Chomsky share a common political program and a common style of violence and vituperation. They are anti-Israel without restraint. While they work with the Left in opposition to Western democracy, and in fact depend heavily on Left support, they are also unashamedly supportive of the neo-Nazis, especially on matters relating to Jews.

And here we have the true significance of the Chomsky phenomenon. Together with Vergès and a handful of other relatively prominent individuals in America and Europe, he has succeeded in rescuing old-fashioned Jew-baiting from the extinction it might otherwise have suffered in the post-Hitler world.

There is one more thing. Unlike Vergès, Chomsky is a Jew, and this fact is surely of some interest. I have been asked by some readers to speculate on the psychology of a Jew who behaves in this manner.

Unfortunately I have nothing to offer that would not already have occurred to the attentive reader. After all, Chomsky is not the first Jew in history, nor the last, surely, to devote his life to this kind of enterprise.

•••

Since the first edition of this work, Chomsky's ties with the neo-Nazi Holocaust-denying *Institute for Historical Review* have been strengthened.

The IHR's publishing and bookselling arm is called *Noontide Press*. Holocaust-denying is only one part of the antisemitic menu of this supermarket of Nazism. The latest *N P* catalog is dated 1995. Among its offerings we find Nazi-made movies that are banned in Germany because of their brazen propaganda (pp. 29, ff), as well as the notorious *Protocols of the Elders of Zion* (p. 10), books by Adolf Hitler and Joseph Goebbels (pp. 10 and 12), a book by the late Father Coughlin (p. 7), and the infamous *The*

International Jew by Henry Ford. Chomsky is represented by five separate items: two audio cassette tapes (p. 26); *The Fateful Triangle* (p. 16); *Necessary Illusions* (p. 11); and *Pirates and Emperors* (p. 12). Chomsky, according to the *IHR*, "enlightens as no other writer on Israel, Zionism, and American complicity." (p. 4).

Since the first edition of this book, also, Chomsky and his friends have produced a further flood of propaganda. There is a "Common Courage Press" in Maine and a "Black Rose Books" in Canada, as well as other enterprises, all churning out propaganda pamphlets by Chomsky and his helpers. *Z Magazine* and *Lies of Our Time*, among others, publish his articles. The Pacifica radio network tirelessly broadcasts tapes of his speeches.[14] Finally, the Chomsky group has been able to appropriate Canadian public funds to produce a hagiographic movie, *Manufacturing Consent*, with Chomsky as subject.

Chomsky has not changed his themes in this avalanche of words. Most of what he has to say amounts to the simple claim that the United States and Israel are to be blamed for the ills of the world.

The Chomskyana that appeared before the current peace negotiations always praised the PLO and its chairman, Yasser Arafat; until very recently, Chomsky was the very model of a Jew for Arafat. But now that Arafat negotiates with the enemy, Chomsky has suddenly turned viciously anti-Arafat. On April 17, 1994, Chomsky spoke at the Berkeley (California) Community Theater saying that "Something's Happening." [15] Suddenly he finds "corruption" in the PLO, a PLO dictatorship, and an Arafat who is selling out. The whole peace process is a joint Israeli-American plot. In the absence of an unconditional surrender by Israel, Chomsky leaves no doubt that he will oppose and denounce any letup in the intransigent Arabs' war against the Jews.

Finally, as we have already seen, Chomsky has recently awarded his urgent recommendation to

Israel Shahak's scurrilous tract against the Talmud and the Jews.

Chomsky will soon enter the eighth decade of his life. Some men and women similarly possessed — Vanessa Redgrave is apparently among these — have seen a decline of inspiration from the Furies as they grow older. But others have become crustier and more and more outrageous. Let us hope, for his sake no less than for ours, that Avram Noam Chomsky, son of a noted Hebrew scholar and himself exposed to Hebrew learning in his youth, will find the peace of moderation as he enters his old age.

•••

The first edition of this book, reprinted here with only minor changes, was published by Americans for a Safe Israel. I owe a debt of gratitude to the people who helped with that edition: Herb Zweibon, Erich Isaac, Rael Jean Isaac, and Frances Besner Newman who designed the original cover. Since AFSI is active in supporting the right-wing opposition to the present (Labor) government of Israel, it has been suggested to me that my book may be identified with that point of view. I do not think that these matters are relevant to the Chomsky issue, but many readers have raised them, and I can see no harm in clarifying my personal position. I am not a member of AFSI, and, unlike AFSI, I am (cautiously) happy about the current peace negotiations between Israel and the PLO.

I have had some personal correspondence with Noam Chomsky in connection with this book. Copies of this correspondence, together with related materials, have been deposited with the Tamiment Institute Library at New York University.

For helping with the new edition, I am grateful to Jon Haber, Hillel Stavis, and Gabriel Schoenfeld.

Finally, the author's share of any profits arising from this book have been assigned to the Jewish National Fund.

The Hidden Alliances of Noam Chomsky

Everyone knows Noam Chomsky of the Massachusetts Institute of Technology for his linguistics and his left-wing politics. But the fact that he also plays an important role in the neo-Nazi movement of our time — that he is, without any doubt, the most important patron of that movement – – is well known only in France. Much like a bigamist who must constantly strain to keep one of his families secret from the other, Chomsky and his most initiated supporters try to prevent his liberal and left-wing followers from knowing too much about his other, his neo-Nazi life.

The Hidden Alliances of Noam Chomsky

Chomsky has said that his contact with the neo-Nazis is strictly limited to a defense of their freedom of speech. He has said that he disagrees with the most important neo-Nazi article of faith, viz. that the Holocaust never happened. But such denials have not prevented him from prolonged and varied political collaboration with the neo-Nazi movement, from agreement with it on other key points, nor — and this has proven essential for the neo-Nazis especially in France — from using his scholarly reputation to promote and publicize the neo-Nazi cause.

Avram Noam Chomsky was born in Philadelphia in 1928. He is the son of the noted Hebraist William (Zev) Chomsky and was educated in the progressive schools of his parents' milieu. Later, apparently because he was thought to be exceptionally brilliant, he was awarded a bachelor's and even a Ph.D. degree in linguistics without going through any required courses or formalities. Today he is Institute Professor at MIT and author of numerous and highly influential books on the nature of language. His work is respected by scholars and admired by the public. It would be difficult to find a more prestigious figure in American, or, for that matter, in international academia.

But if we judge by the treatment he has received in the press, his fame rests most of all on his involvement with the anti-Vietnam War movement of the late 1960's and early 1970's. In the decade from 1966 to 1975 *The New York Times Index* mentioned him a total of ninety-five times, eighty-two times for political activities and the rest for scholarly work.

Since 1976, Chomsky's public notoriety having noticeably declined, the *Index* awards him just twenty-one references, again mostly — in seventeen cases — for his politics. But whether the news item deals with politics or linguistics some mention is almost invariably made to Chomsky's academic status and it seems doubtful that without it his politicking would have been at all newsworthy.

The Hidden Alliances of Noam Chomsky

I have tried to find references in *The New York Times* to Chomsky's neo-Nazi involvements and could find only two items, out of the over one hundred devoted to him, that allude to this side of his activities. The story is quite different in France where *Le Monde* and other publications regularly refer to Chomsky's relationship to the French neo-Nazi propagandist Robert Faurisson. But in America there is little to deflect the casual observer from an impression of Chomsky as an eminently reasonable academic who may, at the very worst, sometimes get a bit overly zealous in his pursuit of the good (i.e. left-wing) society.

One characteristic of Chomsky's political writings that does raise immediate questions about his judgment is his obvious animus toward the United States and Israel. He occasionally says bad things about most of the governments of the world but it is Israel and the United States for which he reserves his extraordinary vitriol. Chomsky is careful not to justify Hitler explicitly but his writings create the impression that the Nazis could not have been any worse than the "war criminals" of the United States and Israel today. Moreover, and this is indeed curious, almost all references to Nazis in his books turn out to be denunciations of Nazi-*like* behavior on the part of Israelis.

But it is well known that Chomsky is Jewish and his anti-Israel stance, when not examined closely enough to reveal its radically malevolent kernel, is sometimes considered as a liberal Jew's way of leaning over backward to be fair to the other side. As for the anti-Americanism, well, that is surely something quite in vogue ...

Chomsky's writings are often praised by his admirers as packed with "facts." And indeed there are many footnotes and many references to apparently esoteric pieces of information. But I have found that these references, at least those that deal with crucial points, simply do not check out. Sometimes the source is impossible to track down, sometimes it is completely misquoted, very often it is so patently and completely biased that no responsible scholar could have taken it at face value. Later in this essay I shall demonstrate these problems by examining Chomsky's treatment of two important episodes in the history of Israel. In regard to Chomsky's treatment of U. S. foreign policy, Stephen Morris has already demonstrated Chomsky's sleight-of-hand methods back in 1981.[16]

But none of this — not his strident left-wing politics, not his bitter anti-Israel activism, certainly not his disreputable scholarship on matters political –– seems to interfere with what still amounts to a very high prestige in wide circles of educated America. It remains to be seen what will happen when his neo-Nazi connections get to be more widely known.

Chomsky and the Neo-Nazis

The name Robert Faurisson represents the most obvious (but not the most significant) connection between Chomsky and the neo-Nazis. Faurisson is a French hate-filled crank, a one-time lecturer in literature at the University of Lyon, right-wing, and deeply antisemitic.[17] As we shall see presently (and although he denies this heatedly), Chomsky seems to have taken to this gentleman and has, in any case, seen fit to keep political company with him.

Faurisson says that he is proud that his writings are distributed by partisans of both the left (*La Vieille Taupe*) and the right wing (*Ogmios*). The fact is that, in each case, these are tiny sectarian groupings. *Ogmios* is a Parisian bookstore-cum-movement that belongs to the antisemitic, anti-foreign, extreme right wing of the French political spectrum. It is reported to have received financial aid from the government of Iran.[18] Far more important to Faurisson is *La Vieille Taupe* ("The Old Mole") under the leadership of Pierre Guillaume, a small group of self-styled leftists who publish Faurisson's booklets and pamphlets, advertise them, publicize them, propagandize for them. It is they who are the friends of Chomsky, and it is through them that Chomsky was recruited to his present position as grand patron of the neo-Nazi movement. (At the time of this writing, Ogmios and La Vieille Taupe have joined forces to publish a new antisemitic review, *Annales d'Histoire Révisionniste*.)

Since the 1960's, Faurisson says, he has devoted innumerable hours to what he considers a very deep study of the fate of the Jews during the Second World War. He has written some books and articles on the subject and summarizes his "findings" as follows:

The alleged Hitlerite gas chambers and the alleged genocide of the Jews form one and the same historical lie, which opened the way to a gigantic political-financial swindle, the principal beneficiaries of which are the State of Israel and international Zionism, and the principal victims of which are the German people — but not its leaders — and the entire Palestinian people.[19]

The Hidden Alliances of Noam Chomsky

Faurisson and his associates on both sides of the Atlantic are pleased to call this Holocaust-denial their "revisionism." They urge, and I cannot disagree, that fair-minded persons in free countries must keep open minds when confronted with reasonable or at least reasoned challenges to conventional wisdom. Perhaps, who knows, Napoleon never existed, perhaps the earth is flat, perhaps the Jews persecuted Hitler rather than vice versa, perhaps there was no such thing as a Holocaust of European Jews. All these nice opinions have their advocates and we shall have occasion to look at some of them in due time. In theory all received truth can and must be constantly re-examined in the light of new evidence, and we should be thankful to scholars and other reasonable men when they can confront us with thoughtful skepticism. But when, on the other hand, an outrageous point is advanced without regard for its truthfulness or for any rule of logic or evidence, when it is made simply to injure and defame, in that case, surely, we are justified in being less than respectful to the would-be "revisionist."

In my preparations for this essay on Noam Chomsky it fell upon me to read what Faurisson has to say and even to correspond with him. I can report that his challenge to our knowledge of the Holocaust does not meet any criteria of moral or intellectual honesty, of seriousness of purpose, of intellectual workmanship. All that is apparent is hatred of Jews and an effort to hoodwink his audience. No wonder he has not found a single scholar to take him seriously. Obviously I do not intend to argue against his thesis myself any more than I would argue with a man who says that he has been eaten by a wolf. But it is necessary to give an indication of the intellectual level of Faurisson's propaganda so that the reader can get some inkling of why he is ostracized by all decent men.

The heart of Faurisson's argument is based on his assertion that Jewish witnesses to the Holocaust are simply liars and that they are liars because they are

Jews. Professor Rudolf Vrba, a colleague of mine at the University of British Columbia, was a witness to the exterminations at Auschwitz and is one of the very few to have survived. Faurisson names him a liar and a Jew and asserts that all who have had anything to do with bringing the Auschwitz facts to light -- witnesses, investigators, magistrates, etc. — are either Jews or, in one case, "probably a Jew."[20] The Jewishness of a witness or writer, throughout Faurisson's opus, is enough to destroy his credibility in Faurisson's eyes. (He does make exception for Chomsky and the two or three other Jews who have rallied to him in a veritable paroxysm of self hatred.)

Faurisson is a practitioner of what might be called the Method of Crucial Source, a favorite among cranks. The Method consists of seizing upon a phrase or sentence or sometimes a longer passage from no matter where, without regard to its provenance or reliability, to "prove" a whole novel theory of history or the universe. More often than

not the Source in question is a newspaper item —
after all, what cannot be found in some newspaper
somewhere, at some time.

Among the many little booklets and leaflets
which Faurisson and his left-wing publishers
distribute by mail and in person, pride of place must
go to a very pretentious pamphlet of twenty-four
pages which contains the French translation of an
interview — a long text by Faurisson interspersed
with a few helpful questions by the interviewer —
originally published in an Italian magazine in 1979.[21]
This short pamphlet has 61 footnotes in very small
print as well as a lengthy footnote to a footnote.
Clearly it represents a major effort at presenting the
gist of what Faurisson considers his proof that the
Holocaust never happened.

One of Faurisson's basic claims is that Hitler's
actions against the Jews were of the same order as
Jewish actions against Hitler, one provoking the
other as it were (p. 15). To prove that there had been

a Jewish "war" against Hitler as early as March of 1933, Faurisson devotes his one and only pictorial illustration in this pamphlet to a reproduction of the front page of the *Daily Express* of London, dated March 24, 1933, which indeed bore a main headline "Judea Declares War on Germany." Sub-heads read "Jews of All the World Unite — Boycott of German Goods."

Now Faurisson claims as his particular specialty the analysis of disputed documents and sources. (As Nadine Fresco has shown, these claims add a touch of lunacy to his malice.[22]) Here he uses the *Daily Express* as his Crucial Source, and, I suppose, the reader who is likely to be impressed by his propaganda may not ask about the nature of this newspaper in those days.

In 1933, the *Daily Express* was a sensationalist mass circulation paper run by Lord Beaverbrook, a man of often eccentric views who felt no compunction about using his headlines to promote

favorite causes or to denounce pet peeves.[23] During
the early years of the Hitler regime he thought that
Britain should avoid alliances with France and other
threatened European countries. In a private letter in
1938, he expressed the fear that "The Jews may drive
us into war."[24] But his most famous pronouncement
of the period, delivered in the very same front-page
headline style as the "Judea Declares War" item of
1933, came on September 30, 1938: "The Daily
Express declares that Britain will not be involved in a
European war this year, or next year either. Peace
agreement signed at 12:30 a.m. today."[25]

To Faurisson, nevertheless, *Daily Express*
headlines represent the most weighty proof of what
happened in history. And so important is this
Crucial Source to the "revisionists" that Faurisson's
California outlet, the "Institute for Historical
Review," sees fit to use it with just a bit of
embroidery of its own: "Is it true that Jewish circles
'declared war on Germany?' Yes it did. The media

the world over carried headlines such as 'Judea Declares War on Germany.'"[26]

Faurisson has been the object of legal challenges because of his strident, exhibitionist, unscrupulous defamations of Holocaust witnesses and respected scholars of the Holocaust. He has also been suspended from his post at the University of Lyon for similar reasons. The court cases, of which Faurisson and his accomplices are inordinately proud because of the tremendous publicity they derive from them,[27] are similar in nature to the Keegstra and Zundel trials in Canada. Here too neo-Nazi publicists have been brought to court under statutes that derive from the law of libel: freedom of speech is held to be no excuse when it can be shown that falsehood is spread deliberately for purposes of inflaming hatred. Faurisson has traveled to Toronto in the Zundel trial as an "expert witness" on matters of truth vs. falsehood, but the jury was not persuaded by him and convicted Zundel.

When freedom of speech encroaches upon or is said to encroach upon other human rights, thoughtful civil libertarians will wish to look at the particulars of the case rather thoroughly. Chomsky says that he sees no need for such concerns, holding that "one who defends the right of free expression incurs no special responsibility to study or even be acquainted with the views expressed."[28] So presumably spreading deliberate falsehood -- say the representation of a consumer product as safe when in fact it is dangerous — would enjoy Chomsky's enthusiastic defense. In any case it is a devotion to freedom of expression, he says, that has led Chomsky so frequently and so energetically to come to the defense of Faurisson. We shall have to examine this claim in more detail presently.

The relationship between Chomsky and Faurisson's publisher, *La Vieille Taupe*[29] (hereafter **VT**), has been chronicled in two remarkably revealing documents in 1986.[30] The first, by far the longer, is a narrative written by VT's leader, Pierre Guillaume; the second, much briefer, is a commentary on this narrative by Chomsky. Taken together, these documents tell us things that might well cause embarrassment among Chomsky's American supporters.

Guillaume begins by telling us that he first met Chomsky some time in 1979, having been introduced by Serge Thion, another member of the VT group whom we shall encounter again. Guillaume told Chomsky about Faurisson at this meeting. Faurisson had begun to have various legal problems. Then, says Guillaume, several months later, and without any other contact having taken place between them, Chomsky signed and promoted the following petition (reproduced by Guillaume in its original English):

Dr. Robert Faurisson has served as a respected professor of twentieth-century French literature and document criticism for over four years at the University of Lyon-2 in France. Since 1974 he has been conducting extensive historical research into the "Holocaust" question.

Since he began making his findings public, Professor Faurisson has been subject to a vicious campaign of harassment, intimidation, slander and physical violence in a crude attempt to silence him. Fearful officials have even tried to stop him from further research by denying him access to public libraries and archives.

We strongly protest these efforts to deprive Professor Faurisson of his freedom of speech and expression, and we condemn the shameful campaign to silence him.

We strongly support Professor Faurisson's just right of academic freedom and we demand that university and government officials do everything possible to ensure his safety and the free exercise of his legal rights.

It is the publication of this petition in French newspapers, with Chomsky's name on top, that caused the first great consternation among Chomsky's left-wing supporters in France and elsewhere. The lamentable Alfred Lilienthal, the only other Jew of any notoriety with antisemitic connections, was also among the first signatories to the petition.[31] Many civil libertarian readers objected to the petition's use of the word "findings" to characterize Faurisson's propaganda, seeing it as an endorsement of Faurisson's work and thereby going beyond a defense of freedom of speech. Chomsky has tried to parry this objection by denying that "findings" means what it means.[32] But it might also be pointed out that the petition describes Faurisson as being, among other things, "respected" for his "document criticism." In fact Faurisson enjoys no such respect unless we count the antisemitic lunatic fringe.[33] In any case, according to Faurisson himself,[34] the petition was originally drawn up not by a neutral civil libertarian but by Mark Weber, an American one-time professor of German who changed careers to become an apparently full-time "revisionist" propagandist.[35]

According to Guillaume, the petition played a decisive role in gaining public acceptance for the "revisionist" movement in France. And most of all, according to Guillaume, it was the prestige of Chomsky's name that helped the crusade of Holocaust-denial.

Next, Guillaume proceeds to tell us how helpful Chomsky has been to the VT movement in other ways. At a time when the VT movement suffered from ostracism on all sides, when, moreover, Chomsky could have published a French version of his *Political Economy of Human Rights* (written with Edward Herman) commercially, without VT involvement, Chomsky nevertheless stood by his friends of the VT and published his book with them.

He, Guillaume, would have understood had Chomsky wanted to keep his distance from the VT in public. But no, Chomsky proved steadfast.

After the appearance of the petition, Guillaume tells us, Chomsky received a great many letters of complaint which he shared with Guillaume. Chomsky told Guillaume that the principle of freedom of expression was threatened by such letters and that he wished to reply to them in a public way. Consequently Chomsky composed a text of approximately 2,500 words, *Quelques commentaires élémentaires sur le droit à la liberté d'expression*, "Some elementary comments concerning the right of free expression." In it he declared that everyone should have the right of free speech, including fascists and antisemites, but that, as it happens, Faurisson is neither one of these. Instead, according to Chomsky, Faurisson is best described as "a sort of apolitical liberal." For reasons that will become clear in a minute, this text later became known as "Chomsky's Preface."[36]

According to Guillaume, Chomsky sent this text to Serge Thion, VT's writer and propagandist, asking him to make the best possible use of it. The text was dated October 11, 1980. On December 6, Chomsky seems to have had second thoughts and wrote a follow-up letter to Guillaume and complained that, the state of hysteria in the world being what it is, the whole fight against imperialism could be sabotaged by a campaign that would associate him with neo-Nazism. (Chomsky was never one to understate the importance of his own personality for the fate of the world.) Therefore, if it isn't too late, Chomsky strongly suggests that his text not be made part of a book by Faurisson.

But, alas for Chomsky and the whole anti-imperialist movement, it was too late. The book by Faurisson, with Chomsky's text as preface, had already appeared. When Guillaume and Thion telephoned Chomsky on December 12, Chomsky's reaction — all this according to Guillaume — was firm, clear, and completely reassuring: he now stood by his preface and declared his letter of retrieval to be null and void.

What a friend we have in Chomsky!

Guillaume next reiterates the steadfastness of Chomsky's support and even confesses that without it the intrepid little original band of "revisionists" may never have grown to its present strength. And all this is so remarkable, according to Guillaume, since Chomsky is being victimized in his own country, the United States, where the imperial ideology of the West has somehow been able to raise its ugly head once again. As a result, Chomsky, according to Guillaume, has had his home audience greatly reduced and his popularity endangered.

Guillaume is not insensitive to the problems posed by Chomsky's ritualistic affirmations that his, Chomsky's, views are "diametrically opposed to those of Faurisson." Yes, but Guillaume understands the difference between a truth and a wink, n'est-ce pas (p. 163, my translation) :

> Each time that Chomsky has said that his opinions remain "diametrically opposed" to those of Faurisson, he has done so in terms that are absolutely incapable of hurting Faurisson; and he has always indicated, by a word or a phrase, that his "diametrically opposed" view was more a matter of opinion than of scientific knowledge.

Guillaume replies here to criticism from one Chantal Beauchamp, who, presuming to be more "revisionist" than he, had objected to 'VT's collaboration with what she apparently regarded as an inadequately neo-Nazi Chomsky. Guillaume can reassure her even further (pp. 167-8, my translation) :

> Chomsky was involved in very taxing struggles ..... Dramatic events were taking

place in the Middle East. His own work — the exposure ... of American imperialism there, of the realities of Zionism and of the state of Israel — took on an immediate significance, something that could lead to practical results. How is this work less important than Faurisson's ... ?

The important work of Faurisson is the denial of the Holocaust. The important work of Chomsky is the struggle against Israel. And the common denominator of these, in the eyes of Guillaume and his followers, can only be antisemitism.

Now comes the most interesting part. Guillaume has told us how close a political friend Chomsky has been, how he had sacrificed self-interest to political principle by publishing his book with VT rather than commercially, how Chomsky's "diametric opposition" to Faurisson did not really mean what it said, how Chomsky's work concerning Israel is part of the same overall cause as Faurisson's denial of the

Holocaust. And now, after all that, Guillaume says that he submitted his report to Chomsky for possible corrections or disagreements. So Chomsky was given the opportunity to tell his story should it differ from that of Guillaume. And it turns out that Chomsky indeed has a demurral that he needs to press, and which Guillaume magnanimously publishes as a sort of addendum to his own report. It seems that Guillaume had gotten one very important point completely wrong. It is not at all true, says Chomsky, that he is less popular now in his own country than he had been in the days of Vietnam. "I cannot accept even a fraction of the many speaking invitations that I receive, and now it's no longer, as it was in the sixties, a matter of speaking to five people in a church. Now there are real crowds at colleges and in the community." That is the sum total of Chomsky's correction. It confirms, in the most direct way possible, the close political collaboration between Chomsky and the French "revisionists."

Not only did Chomsky publish his *Political Economy of Human Rights* with Guillaume's organization. He also prepared a special booklet for Guillaume, not published anywhere else, of some of his self-justifying correspondence concerning the Faurisson affair. This publication, *Réponses inédites*,[37] carries Chomsky's name as author and Guillaume's initials, "P.G.," as editor. Guillaume explains that Chomsky had personally reviewed all translations from English to French.

For his part, Faurisson very frequently uses the Chomsky connection in his ceaseless pursuit of some sort of credibility. Bill Rubinstein of Australia reports that he had originally learned of the Chomsky-Faurisson connection only when an Australian Faurisson supporter flaunted correspondence that showed Chomsky furnishing Faurisson with information and advice.[38] It is just about impossible to come across a French "revisionist" publication — be it by Guillaume,

Thion, or Faurisson himself -- that omits the obligatory reference to Chomsky's patronage. [39]

What does Guillaume's movement do to deserve such warm friendship from the famous linguist of MIT ?

The tiny movement of *La Vieille Taupe*, though having a history of quite different concerns that I will sketch later, seems to be doing little but Jew-baiting these days. Through a micro-empire of publishing enterprises, operating under its own name and such others as *Spartacus*, *Éditions de la Différence*, etc., the movement brings out a flood of "revisionist" and antisemitic propaganda. First and foremost it publishes numerous writings by and about Faurisson. It also features several titles by the late "left-wing" antisemite Paul Rassinier and the notorious "The Myth of Auschwitz" by the German neo-Nazi Wilhelm Stäglich.

Recently Guillaume and Ogmios have started to publish a very pretentiously-presented quarterly journal *Annales d'Histoire Révisioniste*. In appearance this magazine resembles a scholarly publication but its function is to show that the Holocaust never happened. The first two issues contain, among other items, translations of articles that have previously appeared in the California neo-Nazi journal *Journal of Historical Review.*[40]

In the spring of 1985 the movie *Shoah* was showing in Paris and VT's leader Pierre Guillaume, obviously seeking more notoriety, personally proceeded to hand out leaflets in front of the theater. The leaflets denounced the "political-financial" swindle by all those who claim that Jews were killed by the Nazis. As Guillaume tells the story, the incident became the basis of a defamation suit against him brought by the International League Against Racism and Antisemitism.[41]

VT's antisemitism is not confined to Holocaust-denial. It has discovered something it apparently thinks is a very clever find. It so happens that the young Bernard Lazare, later one of the founders of left-wing Zionism, wrote a curious little book in the years before the Dreyfus affair made him a partisan for Jewish rights. This self-hating early book, *Antisemitism, Its History and Causes*, is actually not at all a discovery of *La Vieille Taupe*. It has been used by antisemites and antisemitic movements from the days of Dreyfus to the days of Vichy. It is a curious hodgepodge of accusation and self-accusation, particularly bitter about the Talmud and its alleged influence on the Jews. The book can tell us very little about its professed subject but it has consistently been cited by antisemites as confirmation and justification of their hatred. [42] There is no possible reason for anyone but an antisemitic organization to republish it now. VT has proceeded to issue a new edition over the legal objections by members of the Lazare family and the organization Friends of Bernard Lazare. [43]

The Hidden Alliances of Noam Chomsky

La Vieille Taupe is among the very smallest of the tiny political sects of Paris yet it publishes as if it were a major institution. The physical appearance of VT products is very professional and certainly belies the very marginal nature of the organization. I recently sent a one-paragraph note to the group in which I requested a list of its publications. By return air mail I received twelve books and pamphlets. Eight of these were marked with list prices that amounted to a total of 456 French francs. I estimate the four other items to come to at least another fifty francs, or a total of approximately 500 francs for the material in the package. Since the postage cost a further 148.50 francs, the value of the gift that I received from *La Vieille Taupe* amounts to 648.50 francs, or about $117 in US currency. I am obviously not the only person to enjoy this kind of largesse. I know nobody in the group, as far as I can tell nobody in it knows me, and I did no more than express a simple request for a book catalog. Where does the money for all this come from? *Ogmios*, a bookstore of the extreme right wing which is associated with VT in various enterprises, has been linked to the government of Iran (see above). The source of *Vieille Taupe*'s own obviously substantial finances has so far remained a mystery.

Chomsky has of course been criticized for his involvement with Faurisson and the VT movement, not least within the Left. Chomsky has sought to meet all such objections by saying **a)** that he does not agree with Faurisson but is merely defending freedom of speech; **b)** that Faurisson and the VT are being maligned by opponents; and **c)** that the whole affair is unimportant and should not be discussed. Of these three arguments only the first — the civil rights argument — needs detailed examination, which we shall give it later. The other points can be dealt with more summarily.

Chomsky has persistently misrepresented the politics of Faurisson and VT. In his famous "Preface" he calls Faurisson a liberal.[44] He has also seen fit to praise Serge Thion, Faurisson's associate, as a "libertarian socialist scholar"[45] without mentioning that Thion has for the last nine years or so written lengthy books and articles to the effect that the Holocaust is a Jewish lie. Both Bill Rubinstein of Australia and I have sent detailed proof of Faurisson's antisemitism to Chomsky. I have most recently sent him Faurisson's article which declares all witnesses to the Holocaust at Auschwitz to be Jews and liars because they are Jews,[46] but Chomsky has remained obdurate. To Rubinstein he wrote the following:

I see no antisemitic implications in denial of the existence of gas chambers, or even denial of the holocaust. Nor would there be antisemitic implications, per se, in the claim that the holocaust (whether one believes it took place or not) is being exploited, viciously so, by apologists for Israeli repression and violence.   I see no hint of antisemitic implications in Faurisson's work ...

Rubinstein has published this excerpt from a letter that Chomsky sent him.[47]   As he does routinely, Chomsky objected to the publication of his correspondence but he has not denied either the authenticity or the accuracy of the passage.

Chomsky and his friends ordinarily try to suppress all information concerning his neo-Nazi connections.   The best publicized case of such suppression involves the British linguist Geoffrey Sampson who wrote the biographical sketch of Chomsky in the British publication *Biographical Companion to Modern Thought*. Sampson wrote a laudatory description of Chomsky's linguistics but allowed himself the following few words of reservation about his politics:

...he forfeited authority as a political commentator by a series of actions widely regarded as ill-judged (repeated polemics minimizing the Khmer Rouge atrocities in Cambodia; endorsement of a book — which Chomsky admitted he had not read — that denied the historical reality of the Jewish Holocaust).[48]

Sampson has now told the story of how Chomsky was able, through his influence with American publishers, to ban Sampson's contribution from the American (Harpers) edition of this reference work.[49]

A new book of almost 500 pages, *The Chomsky Reader*, has now been published by Pantheon under the editorship of James Peck.[50] It purports to "[bring] together for the first time the political thought of America's leading dissident intellectual." The work is well indexed. It contains no reference to Faurisson, *La Vieille Taupe*, Guillaume, "revisionism," or to any other topic that might give the reader an inkling of Chomsky's neo-Nazi involvements. The one mention of Thion suggests that this French neo-Nazi is actually no more than a Marxist intellectual.

If Chomsky likes to bad-mouth the Communists from time to time, they, on their part, know how to appreciate an ally and are willing to lend a hand in the cover-up. The Communist magazine *Canadian Jewish Outlook* (now known simply as *Outlook*) ran an article in October of 1983[51] that praised Chomsky's attacks on Israel but completely suppressed any mention of his role in the neo-Nazi movement. Communists are usually sensitive to neo-Nazism but in the case of Chomsky there are obviously other considerations.[52]

I have spoken so far only of Chomsky's connections with the neo-Nazis of France, who seem to have been responsible for his recruitment to the cause. But the "revisionist" movement also has an

American branch and Chomsky has become embroiled on this side of the Atlantic as well.

In its very first volume in 1980, the California-based *Journal of Historical Review* carried an article about Jews by a Doctor Howard F. Stein that turned out to be something of an omen of the journal's future.[53] Even to someone well acquainted with antisemitic propaganda, Doctor Stein's piece must have come as a surprise for the sheer audacity of its malice. And as it happens, Doctor Stein's piece also foreshadowed themes later taken up by Chomsky.

The Journal of Historical Review described Stein as an Associate Professor of Medical-Psychiatric Anthropology in Oklahoma. By now he has written quite a few articles — all in psychobabble — in various fringe journals of "humanistic psychology." He has also lectured at the mecca of New Age psychology, the Esalen Institute of California. And Doctor Stein is Jewish.

In his appearance for the "revisionists" Stein presented a rather straight-forward theory about the Holocaust: it is a Jewish myth. It seems that Jews have always fantasized about a Holocaust, from the very beginning of their history. They have always needed to be victims. Today they fantasize that they were victims of the Germans during the Second World War and they are completely insensitive to the great sufferings of non-Jews, in particular Germans and Arabs. Doctor Stein also refers the reader to an earlier article he had written in which he proposed that Jews are afflicted by a "Samson complex."[54] Like Samson in the Bible, it seems, Jews today are bound for self-destruction and seek to arrange matters so that they can destroy the rest of the world in the process. This is a view that Chomsky has also adopted, as we shall see.

I think that it is an open secret that we have in the United States an intellectual underclass of self-described "academic" journals. These dreary periodicals cater to the foolish vanity of college administrators who wish to see "publications" by their teachers. Stein's articles, looked at purely from the point of view of scholarly competence, must scrape the very bottom even of this material: there is not a shred of evidence to be found in his many pages of jargon and free-floating confabulation. By itself that would be as harmless as is almost all this underclass pulp. But Stein's writings have enlisted jargon-mongering in the cause of spite and hate, and this indeed jettisons them into a category quite by themselves.

Doctor Stein has achieved some international recognition for his contribution to the hatred of Jews. The French journal of the "revisionists," edited by our friend Pierre Guillaume, has published a French translation of the original 1980 article.[55]

Compared to Stein's malice, other JHR articles will seem commonplace. The last issue I received, that of Winter 1986-7, carries the article by Faurisson on Höss that I have already mentioned. It carries another piece complaining about an unjust persecution of the (Nazi) German American Bund in the United States during World War II. A book review tells us that when the Nazis established the Warsaw ghetto, "essentially, the German decision was Jewish, since Jews oppose intermarriages, and insist on their own built-in laws. The Germans also had to fear Polish inspired pogroms against the Jews. The wall prevented that as well." Yes, that's why we need the "revisionists" to set us straight about what happened in history.

Canadian Customs authorities have declared this nice journal to be hate literature and have restricted its import into Canada. Consequently I have been unable to check every issue of it and I do not know how often Chomsky has contributed to it. I do have before me the issue for Spring 1986 containing an article by Noam Chomsky, "All Denials of Free Speech Undercut A Democratic Society."[56] This piece contains about 2,200 words and is reprinted from the *Camera* of Boulder, Col.

Subscribers to the JHR also receive lists of books and tapes that the "revisionists" find necessary for a proper education. Some of this material is signed Noontide Press, which, like the Institute for Historical Review, is located in Torrance, California. My latest Catalogue of Historical Revisionist Books, dated Fall 1986, contains, among other items, the following titles: *The Zionist Connection II* by Alfred M. Lilienthal; *Communism with the Mask Off* by Dr. Joseph Goebbels; and *The Fateful Triangle* by Noam Chomsky. A special book list of Noontide Press dealing with what it calls "Jewish Studies" contains *The International Jew* by Henry Ford, Sr., *The Protocols of the Learned Elders of Zion*, "translated from Russian," *The Plot Against Christianity* by Elizabeth Dilling ("A shattering exposé of the anti-Christian hate campaign propounded in the Babylonian Talmud"), and other such classics.

The Institute also sells two separate tapes of a speech that Chomsky gave against Israel, and here are some excerpts from its publicity for these tapes:

> This lecture ... is, to put it mildly, devastating. In two hours of uninterrupted cannonade directed squarely at U.S. foreign policy with regard to Israel, Chomsky ranges brilliantly over such topics as Israeli imperialism ... the role of the Anti-Defamation League ("... one of the ugliest, most powerful groups in America")/ Media suppression, distortion, hypocrisy, and the "Memory Hole." An intense two-and-a-half hour mini-course on *the* political issue of our age, including Chomsky's answers to audience questions.

I have repeatedly called Chomsky's attention to the Nazis' use of his name and his materials, suggesting that he disassociate himself from these

Noam Chomsky and Israel Shahak at a 1994 rally

Israel Shahak

Robert Faurisson

Noam Chomsky

Mark Weber, author of the petition supporting Robert Faurisson signed by Noam Chomsky. Weber is the current director of the Holocaust-denial organization, the Institute for Historical Review.

Pierre Guillaume, photographed at a Paris rally.

people, but he has just as repeatedly remained obdurate to such suggestions.

Freedom of Speech

As we have seen, Chomsky boasts that he will defend the freedom of expression of anyone, any time, presumably regarding anything, and that he does not need to see disputed material in order to defend its right to be heard and published.[57] Bill Rubinstein has already pointed out that this proposition can hardly be taken seriously since there must be limits to freedom of speech in any society. An immediate example is the necessity for prohibiting commercial fraud. But Chomsky is completely mindless in his declarations for unrestricted freedom; neither fraud, nor defamation, nor public mischief of any sort can deter what he is pleased to call his Enlightenment values. Some of his more extravagant postures on these matters are reminiscent of extremist "libertarians" from Caligula to Charles Manson. We shall look into some of the antinomian sources of his political thought later in this essay.

To Chomsky there is no question that the "revisionist" neo-Nazis should be given complete freedom of speech in Western countries (attempts to restrain them have so far been made only in West Germany, France, and Canada). He never tires of exclaiming that freedom of expression should know no limits, his citation of Voltaire settling the matter to his satisfaction.

I myself have been less than happy with the prosecution of the neo-Nazis in Canada, and I am not convinced that the legal prosecution of Faurisson in France is justified. But the issue is a great deal more complex than Chomsky lets on because questions of both defamation and fraud must be addressed. Faurisson and his followers have engaged in an unbelievable campaign of libel and slander — always couched in very personal terms — against the scholars and the witnesses of the Holocaust. Furthermore, as the transcript of the Zundel trial in Canada has shown, it seems clear that the "revisionists" are motivated by malice and not by any historical conviction. I am fortunately not called upon to vote for or against a gag on these Nazis. But if I were, and if a study of all the details of a given individual case were to convince me that freedom of speech should prevail, I know that I would still be very far indeed from being a friend to the gentleman in question.

As is generally the case when extremists face legal difficulties, the neo-Nazis today have two kinds of supporters: those who wish them well because they are sympathetic to their cause on the one hand, and civil libertarians on the other. Since nowadays nobody likes to be recognized as a Nazi sympathizer, just about everyone who supports the neo-Nazis today calls himself a civil libertarian. The trick is to tell who is who.

There is of course no difficulty to this. We all know civil libertarians. We know who they are, what they do, how they do it. In America they are akin to the founders and leaders of the American Civil Liberties Union, and, like them or not, they are liberal by persuasion, liberal by style and culture. They have a record of defending various kinds of unpopular groups, not just one. They will give legal aid to Nazis but they will not associate with Nazis, will not collaborate with Nazis politically, will not publish their books with Nazi publishers, will not allow their articles to be printed in Nazi journals.[58] On these counts alone Chomsky is no civil libertarian.

Chomsky misleads us when he tells how he was recruited to the Faurisson cause. He tries to create the impression that it was civil libertarians who recruited him: "In the fall of 1979, I was asked by Serge Thion, a libertarian socialist scholar with a record of opposition to all forms of totalitarianism, to sign a petition ... "[59]   The plain truth is that Thion was already a partisan of Faurisson at the time, a man second only to Faurisson himself in the propaganda that declares the Holocaust to be a Jewish lie. Insofar as Chomsky is a political friend of Thion's, and this certainly seems to be the case at least as late as 1987,[60] Chomsky must be considered a political friend of these neo-Nazis and not the disinterested champion of free speech that he pretends to be.

There is also the issue of Chomsky's relationships to the civil liberties of individuals and causes that he particularly dislikes: first those who have dared to criticize him, and second the Jews who are persecuted in Russia and in the Arab world. On these matters Chomsky's record is anything but civil libertarian.

We have seen that the British linguist Geoffrey Sampson, having published some mildly critical remarks on Chomsky in a British work of reference, saw himself banned from the American edition of that work. Chomsky denies that he was instrumental in this ban, but his testimony is not convincing because he also argues in favor of censoring Sampson[61]:

> With regard to a book, readers can form their own conclusions. But an entry in a reference work is something quite different. Readers rely on the reputation of the editors to guarantee that what is presented is accurate, not fabrication and mere slander as in this case; and the editors surely have a responsibility to justify this trust.

Chomsky does not revoke his principle of absolute freedom of expression of everyone. It's just a matter of a little exception that he finds necessary: general books may enjoy freedom, certainly, but books of reference, well, that's an entirely different story. Chomsky is fond of making up obfuscating little rules like that. But who is fooled by that? The record here is very clear: Chomsky will gladly violate his professed principles if it is a matter of silencing his critics.

Are there any other limits to Chomsky's generosity on the matter of civil rights?

Chomsky says that he has been privately active on behalf of individual dissidents in the Soviet Union, but he has never, insofar as I have been able to find out, endorsed or aided the movement to allow the emigration of Soviet Jews. I have written to him about that, and I have also most particularly asked him to intervene on behalf of the Jews of Syria.[62] I was rewarded by a number of vituperative letters from him, but on the matter of the oppressed Jews he has remained absolutely obdurate. So when he tells us that he never refuses to sign petitions on behalf of civil rights[63] he forgets to mention that he does make a tiny little exception when it comes to the rights of oppressed Jews, his own people.

To round out the picture of Chomsky's relationship to Faurisson and the neo-Nazi movement, something needs to be said about Chomsky's repeated assurances that he disagrees "diametrically" with Faurisson, that in his opinion the Holocaust did occur. In fact Chomsky has very few words to say about the subject, but they are words that he uses often. He allowed, by way of an obiter dictum in an earlier book *Peace in the Middle East*, that the Holocasut had been "the most fantastic outburst of collective insanity in human history." Now, whenever his relationship to the neo-Nazis is in any way challenged, he trots out these very same words, quoting himself verbatim, neither adding nor subtracting from this ten-word formula. The abracadabra nature of this declaration carries little evidence of conviction and certainly lacks in persuasive power. Nevertheless, with respect to the historical reality of the Holocaust and when writing for an American audience, Chomsky does not wish to be counted among the neo-Nazis.

On the other hand, as we have learned from Guillaume above and from the published record as well, Chomsky is also very careful not to let this little disagreement with the neo-Nazis spoil his good relationship with them. He wrote to Rubinstein that there is nothing antisemitic about Holocaust-denial; he agreed with Guillaume that belief on his part in the historical reality of the Holocaust is a purely personal opinion — a sort of quirk — and is not to be regarded as implying criticism of the "scholarly" work done by Faurisson.

Chomsky has a well-earned reputation as a vituperative political polemicist. He has a ready store of invective and he is not stingy with it when attacking the state of Israel and anyone to whom that state is dear. But aside from the ten-word self-exculpatory formula that I have shown, Chomsky has never, to my knowledge, seen fit to criticize Faurisson or any other neo-Nazi. His "diametric" disagreement with such people is obviously not something that occupies him very seriously.

Now that we have seen some of the ways in which Chomsky has embroiled himself with the neo-Nazi movement I would like to consider why and how this could have happened. I do not propose to speculate, in the manner of the ineffable Doctor Stein, about unconscious psychological quirks or motives. The public record alone is quite explicit and suggests two roots of Chomsky's current neo-Nazism:

A) There is an old ultra-left doctrine of *malign equivalence* according to which all worldly government is equally evil. Chomsky and his friends, under cover of this neutralist faith, have gone beyond it to suggest that government and society in the West are in fact the most evil of all.

B) Certain embittered assimilationist Jewish individuals have long held that the Jews as a group — their religion, their society, their leadership — are in every way despicable, are authors of their own misfortune, constitute a danger to the peoples of the world. This set of opinions is technically known as "self-hatred" and we shall have to return to it below.

These two tendencies, the self-hatred of some Western intellectuals and the self-hatred of certain Jews, are perhaps unexceptionable when moderate and separate. But Chomsky — it is said that he is a brilliant man — has combined them, twisted them into new forms of absurdity, invested them with all of his academic prestige and all of his physical and mental energy, and he has rarely shrunk from embracing the most extreme and the most hateful consequences.

From Marlen to Faurisson

Faurisson is of course not the first to propose preposterous ideas   or to use pseudo-rational methods in the process. Jacques Baynac and Nadine Fresco have recently reminded us that a certain Jean-Baptiste Pérès denied as early as 1827 that Napoleon ever existed.[64] Today there is a California-based Flat Earth Research Society International, only a stone's throw from our Institute for Historical Review, whose leaflet assures us that it can "... prove [the] earth flat by experiment, demonstrated and demonstrable. Earth Flat is a Fact, not a 'theory' ... Australians do not hang by their feet under the world." There is proof for everything.

It is one of the misfortunes of the left wing, both in Europe and America, to have been afflicted with more than its share of Flat Earthers. Many of these marginal socialist and anarchist illuminati are adepts of the doctrine of malign equivalence, i.e. they see all government as basically "capitalist" including that of the Soviet Union, and they find all "capitalist" rule to be equally reprehensible. The autobiographical part of the new *Chomsky Reader*[65] shows us how

Chomsky has adhered to such doctrines, from his earliest days to the present. But we shall also see how both he and *La Vieille Taupe* have gone beyond this anarcho-Marxist tradition to arrive at what amounts to a justification of Nazi Germany.

Chomsky tells us (in page 14 of *The Chomsky Reader*) that he was fascinated by the "Marlenites" when he was a boy of fifteen or sixteen. This was about 1944 or 1945. Insofar as I can reconstruct it now, this ex-Trotskyist splinter group thought that the war was "phony" and that the Western Allies, the Soviet Union, and the Axis powers were all conspiring together against the international proletariat. All sides represented the bourgeoisie (including the Stalin "burocracy," as Marlen liked to spell it), all sides oppressed the workers, all sides were in every way morally equivalent. Chomsky now says that he "never really believed the thesis, but ... found it intriguing enough to try to figure out what they were talking about."

The Hidden Alliances of Noam Chomsky

I want to linger just a bit on the subject of the Marlenites. On the surface it would seem that there is little similarity between this small band of 1940's New York revolutionists and the Chomsky of today. The Marlenites had strange ideas but they were no apologists for the Nazis, so compared to Chomsky and his French "revisionists" they were models of sanity, of moderation, of judiciousness. But as it happens the Marlenites do afford us some insight, first into the atmosphere of the little radical groups that constitute the lineal forebears of today's left-wing neo-Nazis, and second into the methods of historiography that Chomsky and his friends employ today.

It so happens that I myself had a brush with the Marlenite organization *Leninist League*, as it was then called. It was, at the time, led by the veteran New York splinter-group radical George Spiro. Like all American Bolshevists in those days, Spiro used a pseudonym in the hope of warding off the FBI. (The leadership of the Trotskyist Socialist Workers Party having been sent to jail in 1941, this precaution was not as fanciful as it would seem today.) When Spiro chose his "party name" he wanted to honor his (temporary, as it turned out) heroes and picked *Marlen*, *Mar* for Marx and *len* for Lenin.

My first experience with the Marlenites predates Chomsky's by about four years. I was fourteen in late 1940 or early 1941 when I attended a meeting in Spiro's apartment on the Lower East Side of Manhattan. I had been invited by the Marlenite who distributed propaganda to one of the group's larger rivals, and I can't now remember whether this other group had been of the Shachtmanite or the Cannonite wing of the Trotskyists.

Spiro and his Marlenites struck me as not much different from other Trotskyists in the manner in which they conducted their business except that the group was even smaller and even further removed from the common sense of the world. They seemed to have had an even more intense conviction of being the very small elite that alone knows all the esoteric truths about capitalism, war, the class struggle, the future of humanity. It was a matter of very heavy *Rechthaberei*, of disputatious knowing-it-better.

When I first met Spiro, he had already accomplished a considerable political journey. He had been expelled from the Communist Party and had joined the Trotskyists. He had next joined a splinter group led by Hugo Oehler and Thomas Stamm to found the Revolutionary Workers League, in opposition to the "official" Trotskyist organization. But soon thereafter he had discovered that Oehler and Stamm and in fact Trotsky himself were traitors to the working class, so he had left all these groups, with a very small band of followers in tow, to found his Leninist League and to declare World War II to be "phony." I don't think that the number of these Marlenites ever exceeded a dozen or so.

I went to see Spiro again around 1956, in the same Lower East Side apartment where the earlier meeting had taken place. He told me then that the intervening years had brought him one disappointment after another. His researches had led him to see that not only Stalin and Trotsky had been traitors to the proletariat but that Lenin had been of the same stripe. And even the writings of Marx could not withstand his careful inspection. Spiro (he had by then abandoned his pseudonym for obvious reasons) discovered that yes, old Karl Marx himself had really been nothing but an antisemite in disguise. When I asked him about the other Marlenites whom I had met some fifteen years earlier, Spiro revealed to me that they, too, had been unmasked by him for what they really were, a bunch of antisemites.[66]

Spiro was by then a mellow old man and I must say that I was shaken, not only by his madness but also because of the kernel of truth that his madness all but hid. He gave me a copy of what I take to be his last opus, *Marxism and the Bolshevik State*.[67] I am glad that I kept this volume. At one time in my life I owned other Marlenite literature but unfortunately I discarded it all except for that last big book.

The Hidden Alliances of Noam Chomsky

Marxism and the Bolshevik State has 1100 closely-printed pages, divided into 78 chapters, and gives evidence of a tremendous mental energy on the part of its author. Its thesis can readily be surmised by some of the chapter headings: *The Stalin-Trotsky Betrayal of the British Workers; Lenin Disrupts the Potential World Revolutionary Army and Navy; Marx's Personal and Political Insincerity; A Marxist-Ignored Phenomenon in the Ancient and Medieval Class Struggles — The Jewish Scapegoat; Marxist Antisemitism in the United States; Marxism's Hand in Creating the Reactionary Zionist State; Marxism — The Last Bulwark of Antisemitism and Christianity.* The book denounces all known government — i.e. it embraces the doctrine of malign equivalence — but it also holds open the promise of a new day, when, presumably under the guidance of enlightened leaders like Spiro himself, "Mankind will attain superabundance of the fruits of its labors, will plan its own history, will gradually gain mastery over the globe..." (p. 1077).

Spiro could read German and Russian in addition to English, and he has perused thousands of old books and especially old newspapers, apparently all in the Reference Division of the New York Public Library. Whenever he saw something that he liked he would carefully note it and cite it in his book. As he himself explains the method in his preface:

> In the body of the work for example, we cite a parenthetical remark by Lenin which, to our knowledge, has never been used as source material, and which is of greater value to an investigator of the true history of the Bolshevik State than a shelf of histories produced either by the bourgeoisie or by any historians of that State. (p. 14)

Spiro had no more critical sense about such sources than Faurisson and seemed to think that something printed in an old newspaper, if it tended to confirm his own convictions about history, constituted proof positive of the rightness of his cause. It would never occur to him to consult the work of the expert historians on a given subject, let alone to weigh one source against another. He was a completely self-educated erudite as well as a ceaseless polemicist and self-righteous moralist. Perhaps, had he acquired some sense of balance along the way, he could indeed have become what he thought he had become: an important thinker.

With all that Marlen-Spiro was a rather amiable old crank, and I think that the same can be said for the Flat Earthers, "Marlenites" all. If I now suggest that Chomsky and Faurisson are also adepts of the Marlen method of historiography I must immediately add that Spiro's writings, with all their faults, were free of malice; there was vigorous polemic but there was no hate or vituperation. For these we must look to Professor Chomsky and his neo-Nazi associates.

In any case, Chomsky only gives the faintest of nods to Marlenism in his autobiographical musings. His real political mentors, he says, are Rosa

Luxemburg, Karl Korsch, Paul Mattick, Anton Pannekoek, and some others. [68] These writers are the founders of "Council Communism," and, as it happens, the very ones whom the "revisionist" *La Vieille Taupe* also claims as among its guides and teachers. Chomsky and VT thus have common professed ideological roots, Council Communism, and Chomsky is less than forthright when he suppresses this ideological tie in his autobiographical sketch and elsewhere.

But what is Council Communism? [69]

The beginnings lie in a small sect of left-wing, oppositionist German Communists in the 1920's who were in revolt against Moscow's domination of the German Communist party. Basing themselves partly on the anti-Bolshevist writings of Rosa Luxemburg, the group developed profound differences with the Communist International on organizational matters. It rejected the notion of a "dictatorship of the proletariat" as exercised by a party or state, advocating, instead, independent councils of workers as the government of socialism. Under the influence of writers like Paul Mattick and Karl Korsch (both of whom emigrated to the United States where they died after the war), Council Communists became fierce opponents of Stalin, were persecuted by both Stalin and Hitler, and in general maintained standards of political ethics that were widely admired.

Council Communists were much more consistent than Trotskyists in their opposition to Bolshevist tyranny but they shared certain attitudes with both Trotskyists and anarchists during the Second World War. Wherever they could exist in Europe and America, these little groups and grouplets held to a radical anti-war position; they thought that neither the Axis nor the Allies merited their support. Unlike most of the Trotskyist groups, both Council Communists and the anarchists applied this anti-war position to the Soviet Union as well as to the West and the Axis. But none of these groups, and nobody in them, had anything but hatred for the Nazis. They all supported the resistance in Nazi-occupied Europe, and culturally and practically, insofar as they had any influence anywhere, they were part of the overall anti-Nazi front of all decent people. The current pro-Nazi position of *La Vieille Taupe* is, as far as I know, the first time that a group with authentically left-wing origins has broken this front.

The history of *La Vieille Taupe* has been told by Pierre Vidal-Naquet and Alain Finkielkraut.[70] A group of ex-Trotskyists led by Cornelius Castoriadis and Claude Lefort broke with Bolshevism in the late 1940's to start a movement called *Socialisme ou Barbarie*[71] with ideas broadly resembling those of the Council Communists. Many splits and mergers later, toward the end of the 1960's, one of the resulting grouplets called itself *La Vieille Taupe*. By about 1970, VT began to develop ideas and activities that contrast very sharply with any of its ideological ancestors. It had inherited a thorough-going rejection of "bourgeois" society, and had inherited also a tendency to equate "capitalist tyranny" with "fascism." But now, partly under the influence of certain ultra-leftist Italians (Bordigists), it began to reject the one article of faith that had hitherto been a common denominator for everyone on the left: anti-Fascism.

At first it was a matter of declaring Nazism as no worse than the "bourgeois" capitalism of the West, of finding the Axis as no more guilty than the Allies of crimes against the working class. Such, roughly, were the ideas of the first antisemitic writer whom *Vieille Taupe* saw fit to promote: the ex-Communist, ex-concentration camp inmate Paul Rassinier, now deceased ("Revisionists" from Paris to California still accord him pride of place as the father of their particular branch of "knowledge"). But going from Rassinier on to Faurisson, whom VT discovered in 1978 and has promoted ever since, the group became more and more openly antisemitic and pro-Nazi, a process which reached a sort of apogee in 1986 when it published the 520-page screed of one of the most strident of the German post-War Nazis, Wilhelm Stäglich.

In preparation for this essay I corresponded with some veterans of Council Communism and other far-left wing groups in France and elsewhere. My informants were unanimous in their observations that Guillaume and his *Vieille Taupe*, apart from his two or three tiny front groups, are absolutely and completely alone in this trajectory from anti-Stalinist radicalism to neo-Nazism. As one particularly knowledgeable correspondent put it: "Neither the Trotskyists nor the Council Communists can be held even indirectly responsible for Guillaume's wanderings." Authentic Council Communists will not have anything to do with him. Paul Mattick was one of the respected thinkers of this movement, and his son, Paul Mattick, Jr., wrote to me as follows: "A few years ago, Guillaume offered to publish a French translation of my father's last book, but we (my mother and I) of course refused him the right, as we do not want to be associated with these crazy people."

Estimates of the number of Guillaume followers range from about ten to about thirty. Veterans of the left wing shun him, scholars laugh at him. But Guillaume does have two things going for him. First, as we saw, he seems to have ample finances; second, he has Noam Chomsky.

• • •

The safety and welfare of the State of Israel mean a great deal to most Jews today no matter where they happen to live. There is a minority to whom Israel does not matter much, and an even smaller minority who are critical of both Israel and the Zionist enterprise. And after we have thought of all these categories and try very hard, we can find still others: there is an individual here or there who hates Israel so much that he is willing to aid the neo-Nazis in an attempt to dismantle the State. There is the sad

Alfred Lilienthal, tireless pro-Arab propagandist and speaker at neo-Nazi conventions; there is the eccentric Dr. Howard Stein who translates Julius Streicher's propaganda into psychobabble; and there is Noam Chomsky.

Some individual Jews have always turned against their own people. We call such people "self-haters" after the title of some biographical sketches describing such unfortunates during the Weimar republic.[72] It is of course anyone's inalienable right, in a free society, to be a self-hater, and most such cases are sad rather than interesting. The psychology of how and why a person reaches that stage, especially when that person has had the benefit of every privilege of Western society, is not something that I can claim to understand. All I can do here is to demonstrate the methods, the ways and means, of Chomsky's crusade against Israel and the Jews.

The Hidden Alliances of Noam Chomsky

The Documentary Basis of Anti-Zionism

Chomsky's most ambitious book about the Jews and Israel, published in 1983, is entitled *The Fateful Triangle: The United States, Israel and the Palestinians*. It purports to review the history and current status of the Arab-Israel dispute as well as the role of the United States in it. Like other political writings of Chomsky's, this one has been widely praised by his supporters for its wealth of "facts" and documentation. As we have seen, too, the book is featured as a prized item on the book lists of organized antisemitism.

The violence between Arabs and Jews — who did what to whom and when — is naturally a field of much contention among those who write about the two peoples. Two events in the modern history of Arab-Jewish relations have most particularly demanded the attention of both scholarly and propagandistic writers: the riots of 1929 in Hebron and elsewhere, and the War of Independence in 1948.

Enough about these is known to serve as touchstones for those who would write rationally about Arabs and Jews. I propose to examine Chomsky's treatment of these two events, not only to study his point of view but also to see whether his methods conform to a modicum of scholarly objectivity.

The 1929 Violence

Chomsky devotes two paragraphs of *The Fateful Triangle*, one of main text and one long footnote, to the 1929 events. The text, on page 90, reads as follows:

The [Arabs] never accepted the legitimacy of [Balfour's] point of view, and resisted in a variety of ways. They repeatedly resorted to terrorist violence against Jews. The most extreme case was in late August 1929, when 133 Jews were massacred. The "most ghastly incident" was in Hebron, where 60 Jews were killed, most of them from an old Jewish community, largely anti-Zionist; the Arab police "stood passively by while their fellow Moslems moved into the town and proceeded to deeds which would have been revolting among animals," and a still greater slaughter was prevented only by the bravery of one member of the vastly undermanned British police. (4) Many were saved by Muslim neighbors.*

I have shown the footnote references — one marked (4), the other with an asterisk — as they appear in Chomsky's original. Footnote (4) is found on page 169, and says "Ibid., pp. 109-10, 123," a reference to *Crossroads to Israel* by Christopher Sykes. The footnote marked by an asterisk is found on the bottom of pages 90 and 91 and reads:

* The massacre followed a demonstration organized at the Wailing Wall in Jerusalem to counter "Arab arrogance" –– "a major provocation even in the eyes of Jewish public opinion" (Flapan, *Zionism and the Palestinians*, p. 96). See Sheean, in Khalidi, *From Haven to Conquest*, for a detailed eyewitness account. This provocation was organized by Betar, the youth movement of Vladimir Jabotinsky's Revisionist organization, which is the precursor of Begin's Herut, the central element in the Likud coalition. The very name, "Betar," reflects the cynicism of this fascist-style movement, which, in Flapan's words, described Hitler "as the saviour of Germany, Mussolini as the political genius of the century," and often acted accordingly. The name is an acronym for "Brith Yosef Trumpeldor" ("The Covenant of Joseph Trumpeldor"). Trumpeldor was killed defending the northern settlement of Tel Hai from Bedouin attackers; Jabotinsky "opposed the Labour call for mobilization to help the threatened settlements" (Flapan, p. 104).

Chomsky here acknowledges that a slaughter of the Jews of Hebron had taken place and he borrows words from Sykes to show that this had been "ghastly." He writes the word "ghastly" and his reproduction of the word — though borrowed from Sykes and in quotation marks — may well be used later by him and his friends as proof of his sensitivity to Jewish suffering. As we have seen, Chomsky is fond of such self-exculpating formulas.

But Chomsky is also quick to give us two separate sets of justification for the Arab assassins at Hebron. The first comes at the very beginning of the main paragraph: the killings were part of the "resistance" of Arabs against the Balfour plan for a Jewish national home.[73] The second is more elaborate and takes up the whole of the asterisked footnote: it seems that the killings were "provoked" by a "fascist-style" Jewish youth organization, *Betar*.

How does Chomsky document his charge of "provocation?"

He cites three references in this footnote: **a)** Simha Flapan concerning the import of Betar's demonstration in Jerusalem; **b)** Vincent Sheean, the "eye witness" to the same demonstration; and finally **c)** Flapan again, this time concerning the nature of Betar.

a) Betar's demonstration in Jerusalem: Flapan vs. the historians

Simha Flapan, recently deceased, was a left-wing Israeli editor and polemical writer and indeed says that Betar's 1929 demonstration "... led to the bloody riots and disturbances." But Flapan mentions the incident only in passing, gives no evidence for his assertion, and is in any case no historical expert. Like Marlen, Chomsky here quotes the unsupported opinion of an unqualified writer as if such citation constituted evidence.

It so happens that there is now a scholarly literature concerning the 1929 events and that all such scholarly writing takes as one of its starting points the Report of the Shaw Commission of Inquiry that was appointed by the British government. Chomsky does not mention this Report although it is probably the most detailed description of the facts as they could be ascertained then or now.

One reliable guide to the various claims is contained in Y. Porath, *The Emergence of the Palestinian-Arab National Movement, 1918-1929.* Chomsky professes to respect this work and quotes it as an authority elsewhere in his book (p. 169). Porath takes pains to give an account of provocative actions by both Jews and Arabs in the period preceding the 1929 events. Concerning the demonstrations by Betar, Porath's judgment is as follows:

> While it is true that the demonstration by *Betar* ... at the Wailing Wall on Tishea Be-Av (15th August 1929) prompted the Muslim demonstration there the next day ... the bloody [Hebron] outbreaks occurred a week later and not necessarily in response to the Jewish demonstration. (p. 269)

Porath is known for his sympathies for the Arab national movement, and Chomsky quotes him with approval concerning the Lebanon war on pp. 200, 260, and 334 of his book. But when Porath writes in his most professional capacity, i.e. as a historian of the Arab-Jewish entanglement, Chomsky chooses to ignore him.

Chomsky's failure to refer to Christopher Sykes is equally reprehensible. Chomsky quotes from Sykes in his main paragraph as an authority on the Hebron riots but he suppresses what Sykes has to say in connection with the alleged "provocation" by Betar. Actually Sykes gives a general account of the background in a way similar to Porath. A Jewish boy had been killed in Jerusalem in the days leading to the serious riots. Both Jews and Arabs had been embroiled in provocative acts. Referring to the days immediately before *Betar's* demonstration, Sykes writes that "the atmosphere in Jerusalem was daily growing more tense and the goading policy of the Supreme Moslem Council over the Wailing Wall had the desired effect of driving Jews to exasperation." (p. 136).

In fact all historians agree that Arabs and Jews had been involved in reciprocal provocation, but Chomsky, ignoring all this testimony in favor of the *obiter dictum* of a journalist, sees fault only with the Jews.

b) Vincent Sheean, eye witness

Betar's demonstration of course had hundreds of "eye witnesses." One of these, the American journalist Vincent Sheean, has claimed that his presence at the Jerusalem demonstration qualifies him to pass judgment on what happened a week later in Hebron, where he was not. Sheean tells us that previous to the 1929 events he had been very much pro-Zionist but that the Jewish demonstrations in August of that year, which he blames for all the subsequent bloodshed, turned him into a convinced anti-Zionist ever after.

The Shaw Commission (see its *Report*, p. 52) examined more than twenty eye witnesses concerning the Jerusalem events, of whom Sheean, according to his own writings, was one. Sheean also tells us that his testimony was directly contradicted by others at the Commission hearings, and this is not surprising since eye witness reports are notoriously unreliable. Nevertheless Professor Chomsky cites Sheean and only Sheean as an eye witness, and the question arises why this would be so.

First, a word about how Chomsky discovered Sheean.

Sheean included his reminiscences of the 1929 events, "Holy Land," in his collected essays *Personal History* (1935).[74]   The book was published by standard American and British publishers and is widely available in research libraries. But Chomsky's reference is not to this book. He cites a greatly abbreviated reprint of the Sheean essay in an anthology entitled *From Haven to Conquest*, edited by Professor Walid Khalidi and published by the Institute for Palestine Studies, Beirut, in 1971.

Unlike Chomsky, Professor Khalidi does not profess neutrality between Jew and Arab. He dedicates his volume "To all Palestine Arabs under Israeli occupation" and explains how he selected the various snippets for his book: "Any anthology is selective by definition. The items in this anthology have been selected to illustrate the central theme in the Palestine tragedy, which is the process by which Zionism has sought to wrest control of Palestine and its surroundings from the Arabs." (p. xxiv).

Naturally, materials that do not "illustrate the central theme" are not in the Khalidi book. Chomsky relies heavily on this volume in his own book, citing it over and over again.

One of the ways of evaluating eye witness testimony is to consider whether the witness is credible. Sheean wants to be believed, obviously, not only for what he has seen with his own eyes but also for his insight and perspicacity in relating what he has seen (Jerusalem) to what he has not seen (Hebron). And the unabridged version of Sheean's reminiscences gives us valuable clues indeed about Sheean's credibility.

On pages 409 to 411, Sheean reports "the pogrom heritage" of Jewish people that he observed in Palestine and elsewhere, the unbelievably irrational fear that harm might come to them simply because they were Jews. "It was a state of mind I had never seen before, and it required a powerful effort of the imagination to understand it." (p. 409). But understand it he could not, and what he judged to be

Jewish irrational fears, both in Palestine and in general, are cited as reasons for his remarkable sudden conversion from pro-Zionism to anti-Zionism. He published these observations in 1935, before the Holocaust but already after Hitler's seizure of power in Germany, and of course he was not alone then in his failure to appreciate the exceptional realism of the Zionists of 1929. But alone or not, Sheean's state of mind at the time does not exactly add to his qualification as an informed observer. Perhaps for this reason, these passages are not reproduced in Khalidi's version of the essay.

Sheean's unexpurgated essay also shows great admiration for Al-Hajj Amin al-Husayni, the Grand Mufti of Jerusalem: "But the Grand Mufti kept his head; the better I knew him the more I realized that he was a man of remarkable character, extraordinary inner calm and certainty. He never got excited, he was always open to reason, and he never rejected an argument or a suggestion without examining it carefully." When Sheean published these lines in

1935 he may not have known that two years earlier, immediately after the Nazi seizure of power, the Mufti had conveyed his admiration and support to the Hitler government, praising in particular the Nazi policy of antisemitism. [75] But Sheean should have known, as all informed observers have testified, that the Mufti played an important part in inflaming Arab violence against Jews throughout the 1920s.

Since the Second World War the Mufti has become an embarrassment for partisans of the Arab side. The original Sheean publication must have been among the very last in which a reputable Western writer expressed admiration for him. In Khalidi's version of Sheean, the one cited by Chomsky, all praise of the Mufti is suppressed, as well it might. But without these passages the reader of Sheean is deprived of one of the most important clues to Sheean's lack of credibility.

In brief, Chomsky ignores the scholarly literature on the 1929 riots. Had he reported the contents of this literature to his readers, his pro-Arab and anti-Jewish charges could not have been sustained. He cites the eye witness testimony of only one witness when many were available, and the witness whom he uses has been pre-selected for him by an anthology of pro-Arab writings. Finally, he suppresses all information that would enable the reader to test the credibility of his witness.

Is this the scholarship that is taught at MIT?

c) The "fascist" Betar

Chomsky charges that Betar, the youth organization of the Zionist Revisionist movement, was not only "fascist-style" but actually praised Hitler, presumably as part of its general political stance in 1929. (Of course in 1929 Hitler had not yet come to power and was barely known outside of Germany, but let that pass). Chomsky again cites the left-wing Israeli writer Simha Flapan who had little to say about the Hebron incident but who does devote a whole chapter to Zionist Revisionism.

Chomsky, whose full passage I have quoted above, speaks of Betar as "...this fascist-style movement, which, in Flapan's words, describes Hitler 'as the saviour of Germany, Mussolini as the political genius of the century' .... " Chomsky tends toward forgetfulness in such matters and does not tell us just where he found this in Flapan. The fact is that Flapan wrote something just a little bit different:

The violent anti-labour campaign, accompanied as it was by venomous propaganda, brawls and physical violence on both sides, created in the 1930s a tension resembling a state of civil war [between Labour Zionists and Zionist Revisionists]. The attempt to challenge the labour hegemony failed and boomeranged against the Revisionists themselves. They earned for themselves a reputation as fascists due to the viciousness of the anti-socialist propaganda, their unbridled hatred of kibbutzim, their 'character assassinations', the unconcealed sympathy of some members towards the authoritarian regimes (Hitler, for example, was described as the saviour of Germany, Mussolini as the political genius of the century). — Flapan, pp. 111-2.

Chomsky has Flapan claim that Betar as such embraced Hitler and Mussolini, but Flapan just says that "some members" had such sympathies. The "some members," which here makes all the difference and completely changes the meaning, is suppressed by Chomsky.

Is this how scholarship is taught at MIT ?

But this outrageous misquotation aside, Flapan does maintain that there was some sympathy for Hitler in Betar. How does Flapan know this? To what extent can we trust Flapan as an expert on Betar and the Zionist Revisionist movement? Like Chomsky, Flapan is often cited by Arab and other "anti-Zionist" propagandists. Like Chomsky, Flapan's articles have appeared in journals hostile to Israel. But Flappan's work has a certain inner integrity, and he likes to tell us how he has come to know what he says he knows. So he appends a little note at the end of his chapter on the Revisionists:

> Shortage of time did not allow me to look for and peruse primary sources. Rather, I had to rely mainly on personal recollections of events I have lived through and experienced as a member of the Zionist-Socialist Movement, Hashomer Hatzair ... I have checked these recollections against the official literature of the Revisionist Party.

Those with recollections of the Zionist youth movement some forty years ago will remember, as

Flapan does, that members of Hashomer Hatzair would indeed refer to Betar as "fascist," and that Betar knew how to return such compliments with epithets of its own. What Flapan remembers about such youthful name-calling tells at least as much about Hashomer Hatzair as it does about Betar. Flapan does not cite any direct source, Revisionist or otherwise, for his assertion that even as many as "some" Betar members admired Hitler. And if he had seen any praise of Hitler in the "official literature of the Revisionist Party" we can be sure that he would have cited it. He doesn't.

Flapan is loose about his charge but still stays within the polemical style of 1930s youthful Zionism. Chomsky goes a few steps further. He drops the crucial modifier "some;" he projects back into the 1920's what Flapan describes about the 1930's; he disregards the tenuous and hearsay nature of this evidence. These steps, certainly beyond anything that Marlen would have tried, now give Chomsky his proof that the Jewish demonstrators in 1929 in Jerusalem were really like Nazis.

"The Zionists are like Hitler" and the Question of the Mufti

The Fateful Triangle contains twelve references to Hitler. In each case some Jewish action is said to be like Hitler's or some attribute of the state of Israel or the Zionist movement reminds Chomsky of Hitler.

It is clear that Chomsky is fascinated by Hitler in this book that ostensibly deals with the history of Palestine, with Israel, with the Arabs. With all that, it is surprising indeed that Chomsky has completely overlooked the one political movement in Palestine that openly declared its allegiance to Hitler, the Arab nationalist movement led by Al-Hajj Amin al-Husayni, the Grand Mufti of Jerusalem. By now every school boy knows about the Mufti's great power and prestige in the Arab population of Palestine during the British Mandate, about the

Mufti's admiration for Hitler, about his banishment from Palestine by the British during the Second World War, about the Mufti's state visit to Hitler in 1943, about the embarrassed distance which today's Arab leaders try to maintain from anything that might evoke his name.

There is no mention in Chomsky's book of the Mufti's name or movement, no mention that this movement may well have justified fears among Jews — nothing at all to tell the reader that there ever was a Mufti of Jerusalem who collaborated with the Nazis. Like the Ministry of Truth in George Orwell's *Nineteen Eighty-Four*, Chomsky has consigned the Mufti's name to a hole in which, he no doubt hopes, its memory will be consumed by flames.[76]

Deir Yassin and other Atrocities

Chomsky devotes four pages, pp. 94-8, to a section he entitles "The War of Independence/Conquest."

Much of this section bears no ascertainable relationship to the struggle of 1948, and reports of actual violence are confined to parts of pages 95 and 96. Chomsky introduces this discussion with the impartial observation — self-exculpatory in its judiciousness — that there had been "terror and violence on both sides." But his impartiality vanishes very soon because the only two concrete examples of violence that he shares with his reader happen to be allegations against Jews. First he mentions briefly a Haganah operation at Khissas in December of 1947, reporting the Haganah as "killing 10 Arabs, including one woman and four children." The rest of his section is devoted to events at the Arab village of Deir Yassin.

There are a number of reports concerning this incident of April 8, 1948, but the main facts are not in dispute. Formations of the right-wing Jewish fighting organizations *Irgun Tsvai Leumi* ("Etsel") and the *Lokhamei Kherut Yisrael* ("Lekhi," also known abroad as the "Stern Gang") seized the village and in the ensuing events 254 Arab men, women, and children lost their lives. The behavior of the two Jewish groups was condemned by the official organs of the Jewish community, and Ben Gurion sent a telegram of apology and regret to King Abdullah.

The Deir Yassin episode is reported by all those who write about the history of Israel, but, as we would expect, the treatment varies in accordance with the bias and predispositions of the writer. Jewish and Zionist writers that I have consulted do not seek to hide the horror of the incident.[77] The more-or-less neutral Sykes, recommended by Chomsky for background reading, gives a balanced report and seeks to understand the military motives behind the events. Sykes does not in any way excuse or justify the attackers but he believes their word that the action had been directed against a military post in the midst of the village and that the Arab inhabitants had been urged by the Jewish forces to leave prior to the attack (p. 416).

But be that as it may, all reasonable commentators place Deir Yassin in the context of the ongoing hostilities. Chomsky omits this context completely. He does not mention, for example, that three days after Deir Yassin, seventy-seven Jewish doctors, nurses, and associated university personnel, traveling in a Red Cross convoy, were killed by an Arab ambush. Many similar outrages occurred in the same period, and neutral observers find blame on each side. (Nobody in the Arab world, at least no official source, expressed regret for the killing of the Jewish doctors, or for any of the other Arab attacks on Jewish civilians.)

Chomsky's discussion of Deir Yassin actually has at least three characteristics that distinguish it from any of the variety of fair-minded comment that could be made. First, and in stark contrast to his treatment of Arab terrorism in Hebron and elsewhere, his description of Deir Yassin is one of a totally unprovoked, totally sadistic Jewish atrocity. He comes back to this Deir Yassin "atrocity" throughout the book, mentioning it in all kinds of contexts, always to show the total depravity of the Jewish Zionist enterprise. Second, as we just saw, he completely suppresses the context of violence and counter-violence in which Deir Yassin took place. Third, he treats Deir Yassin as the only military action worth talking about in the War of Independence, thus making of Deir Yassin a myth and an emblem of the whole Arab-Jewish relationship.

Deir Yassin is to Chomsky and his colleagues what Dresden is to those who would justify the Nazis. To the apologists of the Third Reich — and of course they overlap with the "anti-Zionists" — there is only one event in the Second World War that counts: the Allied bombing of Dresden in 1945 and the heavy loss of German civilian life that it entailed. The neo-Nazi Holocaust-deniers refer to Dresden as the only actual holocaust of the War. Dresden and Deir Yassin were terrible tragedies, but the Holocaust-deniers and anti-Zionist s, separately and together, celebrate these events as if their retelling in mythic form constituted a punishment of and victory over the Jews of our time.

Chomsky ends his *Fateful Triangle* by embracing the notion of a "Samson complex." He says that the greatest trouble spot on earth, barring none, is the conflict between Israel and the Arabs.[78] The government and people of the Zionist state, he says, are basing themselves on "the genocidal texts of the Bible"[79] and may well decide to commit national suicide and final destruction of the planet by plunging the world into nuclear war. "This 'Samson complex' is not something to be taken lightly.'"[80]

Chomsky's notion of a "Samson complex," much like that of Howard Stein which we encountered earlier, is in many ways close to the medieval blood-libel against the Jewish people. Stein and Chomsky suggest, partly in so many words and partly by implication, that Jews are exceedingly dangerous beings, that they lack the human qualities of reason and mercy, and that they are possessed by a blind hatred of non-Jewish mankind. Even one of Chomsky's supporters found this Samson doctrine too extreme to swallow.[81]

Chomsky is somewhat more cautious than Stein on this matter. To Stein the Samson complex, insofar as I have been able to understand him, affects all Jews everywhere. To Chomsky it is Israel and its supporters who are to be feared, rather than Jews in general. But like Stein, Chomsky blames Jewish religious traditions, not "Zionism," for this "Samson complex."

•••

I have come to the end of Chomsky's story but there is a final question that some readers may find bothersome. I have described the politics of Noam Chomsky insofar as they relate to Nazism, and I have also shown something about Chomsky's associates:

Faurisson, Guillaume, Thion, the Institute for Historical Review. Chomsky's propaganda, taken by itself, is obnoxious and certainly hostile to Jews but still does not have quite the same character as that of his associates. Where they are frankly neo-Nazi and antisemitic, he fudges and covers himself with self-exculpating formulas. Were it not for his associates we would certainly wish to recognize a line between him and organized antisemitism.

The reader will have to judge for himself what to make of Chomsky's choice of political friends. My summary of the issue is that his associates are in the business of justifying the Nazis and that Chomsky helps them to carry on this business, not at all as a defender of freedom of speech but as a warm and reliable friend.

Much nonsense is sometimes written about the alleged fallacy of "guilt by association." True, if Chomsky happened to be associated with Faurisson and Thion in a tennis club, that particular association would not make him a neo-Nazi. But in fact we saw that Chomsky justified Faurisson's Holocaust-denial, we found Chomsky publishing his own books with neo-Nazi publishers, we saw him writing for a neo-Nazi journal, we saw that the neo-Nazis promote Chomsky's books and tapes together with the works of Joseph Goebbels. It is this complex of antisemitic activities and neo-Nazi associations, not his professed ideas alone, that constitutes Chomsky's war against the Jews.

Notes

1   "The Middle East Lie," *Lies of Our Times*, January 1, 1990, reprinted in Chomsky, *Letters from Lexington*, pp. 3-15.

2   When Shahak staged a particularly fraudulent publicity stunt — he tried to have people believe that orthodox Jews will not save a non-Jewish life on the Sabbath — Rabbi Immanuel Jakobovits exposed him. See Jakobovits's "A Modern Blood Libel — L'Affaire Shahak," *Tradition*, vol. 8, no. 2 (1966), pp. 58-65.

3   Chomsky also contributed an introduction to an earlier pamphlet by Shahak, *Israel's Global Role. Weapons for Repression*, an anti-Israel diatribe published by the Association of Arab-American University Graduates, Inc., Belmont, MA, 1982.

4   References to the older French and American publications will be found in the footnotes to the main text.

5   Karl Marx himself has written an antisemitic essay, *Zur Judenfrage*. On this whole question, see two books by Robert S. Wistrich, *Revolutionary Jews from Marx to Trotsky* (London: Harrap, 1976) and *Socialism and the Jews* (Rutherford, N.J.: Fairley Dickinson, 1982). See also Ruth R. Wisse, *If I Am Not For Myself ... The Liberal Betrayal of The Jews* (New York: Macmillan, 1992), and Arnold Forster and Benjamin R. Epstein, *The New*

Notes

Antisemitism, (New York: McGraw-Hill, 1974).

6   All the varieties of Christian antisemitism, from the beginning to our times, are discussed by William Nicholls, *Christian Antisemitism. A History of Hate*, Northvale, N.J.: Jason Aronson, 1993).

7   Both the Crips and the Bloods, by the way, have now been politicized by the antisemitic Nation of Islam.   See *Village Voice*, August 2, 1994, pp. 24-5.

8   Various splinter groups bridged the institutional barriers between extreme Left and extreme Right. There were, for instance, the National Bolsheviks in pre-Hitler Germany and the movement of Jacques Doriot, the PPF (Parti Populaire Français), in pre-war France. During the war in German-occupied France, leftists of many different persuasions formed grouplets that sought to combine Nazism with Marxism.   Among the most curious of these is the Trotskyist splinter group Mouvement National Révolutionnaire.   It was led by Jean Rous and included a number of Jewish members. It must be said to this group's credit that it existed only a few months, after which its members joined the Resistance. (Personal communication by William Petersen; see also Jean-Pierre Cassard, *Les Trotskyistes en France Pendant La Deuxième Guerre Mondiale*, Paris, La Vérité, n.d., pp. 65-6.)

9   One book that describes all such groups in France,

Notes

including Chomsky's friends of the "Vieille Taupe," is Christophe Bourseiller,1989, *Les Ennemis du Système*, Paris, Robert Laffont. The book by Ray Hill, 1988, The Other Face of Terror, Inside Europe's Neo-Nazi Network (London, Grafton) focuses on the right wing but also provides information on Third Position groups.

10 Cohn, Werner, 1991, "From Victim to Shylock and Oppressor: The New Image of the Jew in the Trotskyist Movement," *Journal of Communist Studies*, vol. 7, no. 1 (March), pp. 46-68.

11 For the Vergès story, see Erna Paris, 1985, *Unhealed Wounds: France and the Klaus Barbie Affair*. Toronto, Methuen. (Unfortunately, this book was published before the completion of the Barbie trial.)

12 Ibid., p. 140.

13 *New York Times*, August 22, 1994.

14 On Pacifica's record of antisemitism, see *The Jewish Week*, August 5-11, 1994.

15 The speech was broadcast on April 17 on Pacifica's station KPFK. My text comes from a transcript of this broadcast.

16 Morris, Stephen, "Chomsky on U. S. Foreign Policy," *Harvard International Review*, Dec.-January 1981, pp. 3-5, 26-31. Responses by readers and rebuttal in

issue of April-May, 1981, pp. 22-26. The article is a review of Chomsky, Noam, and Edward S. Herman, 1979, *The Political Economy of Human Rights*, 2 volumes, Montreal, Black Rose Books.

[17]   What the French neo-Nazis have to say about themselves may be gleaned from the writings by Faurisson, Guillaume, and Thion which are mentioned in these notes. But there are also three excellent major studies of these people, and I am happy to acknowledge my great debt to the following: 1) Finkielkraut, Alain, 1982, *L'avenir d'une négation*, Paris, Seuil; 2) Fresco, Nadine, "Les redresseurs de Morts," *Les Temps Modernes*, no. 407, June 1980, pp. 2150-2211; 3) Vidal-Naquet, Pierre, 1987, *Les Assassins de la mémoire*, Paris, Seuil. As far as I know, only the latter two items have appeared in English translation, Fresco's piece as an exerpt in *Dissent* for Fall 1981. Vidal-Naquet's book has been published in English by Columbia University Press (1992) and excerpted in *Democracy* for April 1981, pp. 67-95. I have not seen these translations and do not know how adequate they may be. There is an excellent article about the American wing of this "revisionist" movement: Dawidowicz, Lucy S., 1980, "Lies About the Holocaust," *Commentary*, vol. 70, No. 6, December, pp. 31-37. We also have a good report by the Anti-Defamation League of B'nai B'rith, 1980, "Holocaust 'Revisionism': A Denial of History," *Facts*, vol. 26, no. 2, June. Credit for the first treatment of the relationship

Notes

between Chomsky and the neo-Nazis, written at a time when many of the materials that we have now were still unavailable, must go to W. D. Rubinstein, "Chomsky and the Neo-Nazis," *Quadrant* (Australia), October 1981, pp. 8-14. A reply by Chomsky and a rebuttal by Rubinstein are published in the April 1982 issue of the same journal.

18 *L'Express*, September 4, 1987, pp. 30-1.

19 Faurisson, Robert, 1985, "Revisionism on Trial: Developments in France, 1979-1983," *Journal of Historical Review*, vol. 6, no. 2, pp. 133-182. This creedal affirmation, comprising sixty words in its original French, is frequently cited and recited verbatim by Faurisson and his followers. For the French version and its ritualistic use, see the pamphlet by Faurisson's chief follower Pierre Guillaume, 1986, *Droit et Histoire*, Paris, La Vieille Taupe, pp. 18-19, 92.

20 Faurisson, Robert, 1986-7,"How the British Obtained the Confessions of Rudolf Höss," *The Journal of Historical Review*, vol. 7, no. 4, pp. 389-403.

21 Faurisson, Robert, n.d., *L'affaire Faurisson*. Interview de Robert Faurisson à Storia illustrata, août 1979. Introduction by Faurisson and notice that this text was revised for the purpose of the pamphlet. There is no date, but the appended book list has items dated as late as 1986.

Notes

22 Op. Cit.

23 Allen, Robert, 1983, *Voice of Britain. The Inside Story of the Daily Express*, Cambridge, Patrick Stephens; Taylor, A.J.P., 1972, Beaverbrook, London, Hamish Hamilton.

24 Taylor, op. cit. p. 387.

25 There is a picture of this front page in Allen, op. cit., p. 66.

26 I am translating from a French-language 2-page leaflet, a catechism, entitled *66 Questions & Réponses sur l'holocauste*, n.d., Institute for Historical Review.

27 Cf. Faurisson's 1985 article, cited above.

28 Chomsky, Noam, 1981, "The Faurisson Affair, His Right to Say It," *The Nation*, February 28, pp. 231-4.

29 The name means "The Old Mole," an allusion to Marx who borrowed the image from Shakespeare in order to rejoice in what he thought was an underground presence of the revolution.

30 Guillaume, Pierre, 1986, *Droit et Histoire*, Paris, La Vieille Taupe. The two documents are published together under the title "Une Mise au Point," 'A Clarification,' on pp. 152-72.

Notes

31   Thion, Serge, 1980, *Vérité Historique ou Vérité Politique?*, Paris, La Vieille Taupe, p. 163.

32 In the *Nation* article cited above. He also takes up the point in his famous Preface, cited as Faurisson, 1980, below.

33   Nadine Fresco' excellent article, cited above, discusses Faurisson's ludicrous claims to expertise in this field.

34 Faurisson 1985, pp. 180-1.

35   Because of his "revisionist" propaganda, Weber became an embarrassment to the University of Tulsa, where he was teaching German, and had his tenure terminated by a cash settlement. See Hill, L. E., n.d., *A 1985 Trial of an Antisemite and Holocaust-Denier in Canada: Ernst Zundel*, ms. in preparation. I am greatly indebted to my colleague Professor Hill for access to a first draft of this important study of the first Zundel trial. Weber, like Faurisson and other "revisionist" luminaries, was a defense witness at this trial and his background became part of the trial record.

36 As far as I know this text has never appeared in English, but the content is very similar to Chomsky's *Nation* article cited above. The French text forms the preface to Faurisson, Robert, 1980, *Mémoire en Défense*, Paris, La Vieille Taupe.

Notes

37   Chomsky, Noam, 1984, *Réponses inédites*, Paris, Spartacus.

38   See the Rubinstein article cited above, as well as the subsequent letters to the editor, cited in the same footnote. Chomsky never challenged the authenticity of the document or the information it contained.   The same document was published as Faurisson, Robert, 1980, "Letter to the 'New Statesman,'" *Journal of Historical Review*, vol. 1, no. 2, pp. 157-161.

39   See, for example, Faurisson, n.d., p. 24; Faurisson 1985, p. 181; Faurisson 1986, p. 69; Thion 1980, p. 163.

40   Faurisson's previously-cited article on Höss (1986-7) appeared in a French version in the first issue of the *Annales*, but there is a very curious bowdlerization. In the American version Faurisson accuses the Auschwitz witnesses of being liars because they are Jews, but this French version makes no such claim. Could it be that there are some kinds of antisemitism that are too blatant even for Monsieur Guillaume? See Faurisson, Robert, 1987, "Comment les Britanniques ont obtenu les aveux de Rudolf Höss, commandant d'Auschwitz," *Annales d'Histoire Révisionniste*, no. 1, Printemps, pp. 137-152.

41   Guillaume, 1986, pp. 9, ff.

Notes

42 Wilson, Nelly, 1978, *Bernard-Lazare*, Cambridge, Cambridge University Press. See pages 90-1 and passim.

43 Lazare, Bernard, 1985, (Original edition 1984,) *L'Antisémitisme, Son Histoire et ses Causes.* Paris, La Vieille Taupe.

44 "Pour autant que je puisse en juger, Faurisson est une sorte de libéral relativement apolitique." Chomsky in *Faurisson* 1980, pp. XIV-XV.

45 Chomsky, 1981, p. 231; see also Chomsky, Noam, 1987, *The Chomsky Reader*, James Peck, editor, New York, Pantheon, p. 294.

46 Cohn to Chomsky, November 18, 1987. I sent him a copy of *Faurisson*, 1986-7.

47 Rubinstein, 1981, p. 12.

48 Cited in Sampson, Geoffrey, 1984, "Censoring '20th Century Culture': the Case of Noam Chomsky," *New Criterion*, vol. 3, no. 2, pp. 7-16. Chomsky's vituperative reply, with a rejoinder from Sampson, appeared in the January 1985 issue of the same journal.

49 Ibid.

50 Chomsky 1987.

Notes

51 Epstein, Norman, 1983, "Chomsky, Israel and Nuclear War," *Canadian Jewish Outlook*, vol. 21, no. 9, Oct., pp. 17-8.

52 The Communist press in Canada, when it still functioned, regularly advertised Chomsky's books and the Communist book store features them together with the works of Gorbachev.

53 Stein, Howard F., 1980, "The Holocaust, and the Myth of the Past as History," *Journal of Historical Review*, vol. 1, no. 4, Winter, pp. 309-322.

54 Stein, Howard F., 1980, "The Holocaust, and the Myth of the Past as History," *Journal of Historical Review*, vol. 1, no. 4, Winter, pp. 309-322.

55 Stein, Howard F., "L'Holocauste et le mythe du passé comme histoire," *Annales d'Histoire Révisionniste*, no. 2, Été, pp. 11-26.

56 Chomsky, Noam, 1986, "All Denials of Free Speech Undercut a Democratic Society," *Journal of Historical Review*, vol. 7, no. 1, Spring, pp. 123-127.

57 See, for example, Chomsky 1981, p. 232.

58 The late Norman Thomas, one of the founding members of the American Civil Liberties Union, was often called on to defend freedom of speech for the

Notes

Communists. When invited to a dinner in honor of the Communist leader William Z. Foster, he replied indignantly: "... I certainly don't want him in jail but neither do I want to sponsor any dinner in his honor. You surely know my position which is that I am supporting your case because of my general views on civil liberties and not because of my sympathy with Communism. I will be honest with you and tell you that I would be a Christian of a rather unusual type if I should be on [Foster's] committee ..." See Swanberg, W. A., *Norman Thomas*, New York, Scribner's, p. 384.

59   Chomsky 1981, p. 231.

60   Chomsky 1987, p. 294.

61   See previous reference to Sampson's article. This passage comes from Chomsky's reply, published in *The New Criterion* of January 1985, pp. 81-4.

62   Cohn to Chomsky, November 2, 1985.

63   See, for example, Chomsky 1984, p. 41.

64   *Le Monde*, June 18, 1987. The Bibliothèque Nationale in Paris has several editions of Pérès but I was unable to borrow a copy on this side of the Atlantic. The booklet, *Comme quoi Napoléon n'a jamais existé*, was republished several times until what appears to be its last edition of 1909. But with all that — and

perhaps this should be a warning to Faurisson — Pérès is not even a footnote in any of the books on Napoleon that I have been able to consult.

65   Chomsky, 1987, pp. 3-55.

66   An old record album *Ballads for Sectarians* by Billy Friedland and Joe Glazer, circa 1951, has devoted a satiric ballad to Spiro, whom they call Bill Bailey. Some of the lyrics, reproduced here with permission of Professor William H. Friedland, went as follows:

Bill Bailey belonged to every radical party that ever came to be,/Till he finally decided to start his own party so he wouldn't diasgree/He got himself an office with a sign outside the door, with "Marxist League" in letters red/ ... / For seventeen years, Bill Bailey kept his office with the sign outside the door./ But he never, ever, got a new member; everybody made him sore./ .../

And so on that day, Bill Bailey passed away, and his soul to Red Heaven flew/He was met at the gate by Old Karl Marx and Friedrich Engels, too./They said. "welcome comrade" as they opened the gate to let Bill come inside,/As he slammed the door back in old Karl's face, these were the words he cried:/"Oh you may be a friend of Karl Kautsky, and a pal of Ferd Lassalle/You may get along with Wilhelm Liebknecht and the First Internationale,/Yes, you may have inspired every radical party from the Hudson to the Rhine,/Oh, you may be a comrade of all of these folks, but you ain't no comrade of mine."

67 Spiro, George, 1951, *Marxism and the Bolshevik State.* "Workers Democratic World Government Versus National-Burocratic [sic] 'Soviet' and Capitalist Regimes." New York, Red Star Press.

68 Chomsky, 1987, pp. 7, 22-3, 29.

69 There is a succinct sketch of Council Communism in Biard, Roland, 1978, *Dictionnaire de l'extrême-gauche de 1945 à nos jours,* Paris, Pierre Belfond, pp. 115-9. Among the works available in English are the following: Kellner, Douglas, ed., 1977, Karl Korsch: *Revolutionary Theory,* Austin, Univ. of Texas Press; Mattick, Paul, 1978, *Anti Bolshevik Communism,* White Plains, N.Y., M. E. Sharpe.

70 Vidal-Naquet pp. 155, ff.; Finkielkraut pp. 40, ff. There is also a very lengthy but quite interesting insider's description that comes to us from one of the tiny splinters that left VT over Faurisson and other matters: (Anon.), 1983, "Le roman de nos origines," *La Banquise,* No. 2, pp. 3-60.

71 On this group, see the recapitulation by Paul Mattick, Jr. (son of one of the founders of Council Communism), 1985, "Socialisme ou Barbarie," in

Notes

Robert A. Gorman, ed., *Biographical Dictionary of Neo-Marxism*, Greenwood Press, Westport, CT.

72   Lessing, Theodor, 1930, *Der jüdische Selbsthass, Jüdischer Verlag*, Berlin. See also a new biography of its author: Marwedel, Rainer, 1987, *Theodor Lessing 1872-1933: Eine Biographie. Darmstadt*, Luchterhand.

73   Chomsky here echoes the position of the Communist International at the time, which, on orders from the Soviet government, gave its support to the Arab rioters in 1929.   Many Jewish Communists were outraged and left the Party over this issue. See Melech Epstein, n.d., *The Jew and Communism*, New York, Trade Union Sponsoring Comm., pp. 223, ff. It is also of some interest here that Albert Einstein, until this point an honorary officer of the Communist-controlled Anti-Imperialist League, resigned in protest over this matter in a letter dated September 6, 1929 (Document 47 458, Einstein Archive, cited by permission of the Hebrew University of Jerusalem, Israel).

74   I have relied on the apparently identical British edition *In Search of History*.

75   Nicosia, Francis R., 1985, *The Third Reich and the Palestine Question*, Austin, Tex., pp. 85-6.

76   How the Mufti is treated may well be used as a quick test of veracity for any book that professes to

discuss Arab-Jewish relations. (Another test is is the treatment of Deir Yassin, see my text below). Here is a report on some of the books that Chomsky cites as his sources: Sykes mentions the pro-German activities of the Mufti very briefly, but he tells the reader what he needs to know. Porath's volume only deals with the period to 1929, but the reader is fully informed about the Mufti's anti-Jewish activities until then and his share in responsibility for the 1929 violence (see p. 270 and passim.). Flapan, though often cited by Arabs because of his extreme views on certain issues, gives the essential facts as well. The 1983 volume by Lenni Brenner, a self-professed Jewish anti-Zionist with Trotskyist views, acknowledges the facts but blames the Zionists: "The Mufti was an incompetent reactionary who was driven into his antisemitism by the Zionists" (p. 102). (Brenner and his work are described in Walter Laqueur, 1987, "The Antisemitism of Fools," *New Republic*, November 2, pp. 33-39.) The suppression of fact begins with the Khalidi volume, which, as we have seen, makes no pretense at impartial scholarship. It mentions the Mufti as a pre-war leader of Arabs but gives no hint about the antisemitism or the Nazi connections. But at least he still exists. For the Mufti's complete excision from history we have to wait until we come to the work of Noam Chomsky himself. Perhaps it is apt that Chomsky published his book just one year shy of Nineteen Eighty-Four.

Notes

77 See the appropriate articles as listed in the index to the *Encyclopaedia Judaica*, and the very helpful *Myths and Facts*, issued every three years by *Near East Report*.

78 Chomsky, 1983, p. 449.

79 Ibid., p. 444.

80 Ibid., p. 467.

81 Epstein, Norman op. cit.

Allen, Robert. 1983. *Voice of Britain. The Inside Story of the Daily Express*. Cambridge: Patrick Stephens.

Anon. 1983. "Le roman de nos origines," *La Banquise*. no. 2, pp. 3-60.

Anti-Defamation League of B'nai B'rith. 1980. "Holocaust 'Revisionism': A Denial of History," *Facts*. vol. 26, no. 2, June.

Baynac, Jacques, and Nadine Fresco. 1987. "Comment s'en débarrasser ?" *Le Monde*. June 18.

Biard, Roland. 1978. *Dictionnaire de l'extrême-gauche de 1945 à nos jours*. Paris, Pierre Belfond.

Bourseiller, Christophe. 1989. *Les Ennemis du Système*. Paris: Robert Laffont.

Brenner, Lenni. 1983. *Zionism in the Age of the Dictators*. Westport, Ct.: Lawrence Hill.

Cassard, Jean-Pierre. n.d., *Les Trotskystes en France Pendant La Deuxième Guerre Mondiale*. Paris: La Vérité.

Chomsky, Noam. 1981. "The Faurisson Affair, His Right to Say It," *Nation*. April 28, pp. 231-4.

Chomsky, Noam. 1983. *The Fateful Triangle. The Unites States, Israel and the Palestinians*. Boston: South End Press.

References Cited

Chomsky, Noam. 1984. *Réponses inédites*. Paris: Spartacus.

Chomsky, Noam. 1986. "All Denials of Free Speech Undercut a Democratic Society," *Journal of Historical Review*. vol. 7, no. 1, Spring, pp. 123-127.

Chomsky, Noam. 1987. *The Chomsky Reader*. James Peck, editor, New York: Pantheon.

Chomsky, Noam. 1992. *Chronicles of Dissent*. Monroe, Maine: Common Courage Press.

Chomsky, Noam. 1993. *Letters from Lexington*. Monroe, Maine: Common Courage Press.

Chomsky, Noam, and Edward S. Herman.1979. *The Political Economy of Human Rights*. 2 volumes, Montreal: Black Rose Books.

Cohn, Werner. 1991. "From Victim to Shylock and Oppressor: The New Image of the Jew in the Trotskyist Movement," *Journal of Communist Studies*. vol.7, no. 1 (March), pp. 46-68.

Commission on the Palestine Disturbances. 1930. *Report*. London: H.M. Stationery Office, Cmd. 3530. [SHAW REPORT}

References Cited

Dawidowicz, Lucy S. 1980 "Lies About the Holocaust," *Commentary*. vol. 70, No. 6, December, pp. 31-37.

Epstein, Melech, n.d. *The Jew and Communism*. New York: Trade Union Sponsoring Committee.

Epstein, Norman. 1983. "Chomsky, Israel and Nuclear War," *Canadian Jewish Outlook*. vol. 21, no. 9, Oct., pp. 17-8.

Faurisson, Robert. 1980. "Letter to the 'New Statesman,'" *Journal of Historical Review*. vol. 1, no. 2, pp. 157-161.

Faurisson, Robert. 1980. *Mémoire en Défense*. Paris, La Vieille Taupe. Préface de Noam Chomsky.

Faurisson, Robert. 1985. "Revisionism on Trial: Developments in France, 1979-1983," *Journal of Historical Review*. vol. 6, no. 2, pp. 133-182.

Faurisson, Robert. 1986. "Response to a Paper Historian," *Journal of Historical Review*. vol. 7, no. 1, pp. 21-72.

Faurisson, Robert. 1986-7. "How the British Obtained the Confessions of Rudolf Höss," *Journal of Historical Review*. vol. 7, no. 4, pp. 389-403.

References Cited

Faurisson, Robert. 1987. "Comment le Britanniques ont obtenu les aveux de Rudolf Höss, commandant d'Auschwitz," *Annales d'Histoire Révisionniste*. no. 1, Printemps, pp. 137-152.

Faurisson, Robert, n.d., *L'affaire Faurisson*, Interview de Robert Faurisson à *Storia illustrata*. août 1979, no. 261. (Pamphlet published by La Vieille Taupe, Paris.)

Finkielkraut, Alain. 1982. *L'avenir d'une négation*. Paris: Seuil.

Flapan, Simha. 1979. *Zionism and the Palestinians*. London: Croom Helm.

Fresco, Nadine. 1980. "Les redresseurs de Morts," *Les Temps Modernes* no. 407, (June), pp. 2150-2211. English version (partial ?) in *Dissent*, Fall 1981.

Guillaume, Pierre. 1986. *Droit et Histoire*. Paris: La Vieille Taupe

Hill, L. E., n.d., "The Trial of Ernst Zundel: Revisionism and the Law in Canada" *Simon Wiesenthal Center Annual*, Vol. 6, pp. 165-219.

Hill, Ray. 1988. *The Other Face of Terror. Inside Europe's Neo-Nazi Network*. London: Grafton.

Jakobovits, Immanuel. 1966. "A Modern Blood Libel -- L'Affaire Shahak," *Tradition*. vol. 8, no. 2, pp. 58-65.

Kellner, Douglas, ed. 1977. *Karl Korsch: Revolutionary Theory*. Austin: University of Texas Press.

Khalidi, Walid, edit. 1971. *From Haven to Conquest*. Beirut: Institute for Palestine Studies.

Laqueur, Walter. 1987. "The Anti-Semitism of Fools," *New Republic*. November 2, pp. 33-39.

Lessing, Theodor. 1930. *Der jüdische Selbsthass*. Berlin: Jüdischer Verlag.

Marwedel, Rainer. 1987. *Theodor Lessing 1872-1933: Eine Biographie*. Darmstadt: Luchterhand.

Marx, Karl. 1844 (1982). "Zur Judenfrage," in *Karl Marx, Friedrch Engels Gesamtausgabe (MEGA)*. Erste Abteilung, Band 2. Berlin: SED

Mattick, Paul, Jr. 1985. "Socialisme ou Barbarie," in Robert A. Gorman, ed., *Biographical Dictionary of Neo-Marxism*. Westport, Ct.: Greenwood Press.

Mattick, Paul 1978. *Anti Bolshevik Communism*. White Plains, N.Y.: M.E. Sharpe.

Morris, Stephen. 1981. "Chomsky on U. S. Foreign Policy," *Harvard International Review*. Dec.-January, pp. 3-5, 26-31. Responses by readers and rebuttal by Morris in issue of April-May, 1981, pp. 22-26.

References Cited

Near East Report. *Myths and Facts*, triannual periodical, Washington.

Nicholls, William. 1993. *Christian Antisemitism. A History of Hate*. Northvale, NJ: Jason Aronson.

Nicosia, Francis R. 1985 *The Third Reich and the Palestine Question*. Austin, Tex: Univ. of Texas Press.

Paris, Erna. 1985. *Unhealed Wounds. France and the Klaus barbie Affair*. Toronto: Methuen.

Porath, Y. 1974 *The Emergence of the Palestinian-Arab National Movement, 1918-1929*. London: Frank Cass.

Rubinstein, W. D. 1981 "Chomsky and the Neo-Nazis," *Quadrant* (Australia), October, pp. 8-14. A reply by Chomsky and a rebuttal by Rubinstein are published in April 1982 issue of the same journal.

Sampson, Geoffrey. 1984. "Censoring '20th Century Culture': the Case of Noam Chomsky," *New Criterion*. vol. 3, no. 2, pp. 7-16. Chomsky's, with a rejoinder from Sampson, appeared in the January 1985 issue of the same journal.

Shahak, Israel. 1982. *Israel's Global Role: Weapons for Repression*. Introduction by Noam Chomsky. Belmont, Mass.: Association of Arab-American University Graduates.

Shahak, Israel. 1994. *Jewish History, Jewish Religion.* Foreword by Gore Vidal. Cover blurb by Noam Chomsky. London: Pluto Press.

Sheean, Vincent. 1935. *In Search of History.* London: Hamish Hamilton.

Spiro, George. 1951. *Marxism and the Bolshevik State. Workers Democratic World Government Versus National-Burocratic* [sic] *'Soviet' and Capitalist Regimes.* New York: Red Star Press.

Stein, Howard F. 1978 "Judaism and the Group-Fantasy of Martyrdom: The Psychodynamic Paradox of Survival Through Persecution," *The Journal of Psychohistory.* pp. 151-210.

Stein, Howard F. 1980. "The Holocasut, and the Myth of the Past as History," *Journal of Historical Review.* vol. 1, no. 4, Winter, pp. 309-322.

Stein, Howard F. 1987. "L'Holocauste et le mythe du passé comme histoire," *Annales d'Histoire Révisionniste.* no. 2, Été, pp. 11-26.

Swanberg, W. A. *Norman Thomas.* New York: Scribner's.

Sykes, Christopher. 1965. *Cross Roads to Israel.* London: Collins. DS 125 S86 1965.

References Cited

Taylor, A.J.P. 1972. *Beaverbrook*. London: Hamish Hamilton, p. 387.

Thion, Serge, 1980, Vérité Historique ou Vérité Politique ?, Paris, La Vieille Taupe.

Vidal-Naquet, Pierre. 1987. *Les Assassins de la mémoire*. Paris: Seuil. Partial English translation in *Democracy*, April 1981, pp. 67-95.

Wilson, Nelly, 1978. *Bernard-Lazare*. Cambridge: Cambridge University Press.

Wisse, Ruth R. 1992. *If I am Not for Myself ... The Liberal Betrayal of the Jews*. New York: Macmillan.

Wistrich, Robert S. 1976. *Revolutionary Jews from Marx to Trotsky*. London: Harrap.

Wistrich,Robert S. 1982. *Socialism and the Jews*. Rutherford, NJ: Fairly Dickinson.

Index

al-Husayni, Al-Hajj Amin, 118, 125
Annales d'Histoire Révisioniste, 44, 65
anti-Zionism, 15, 108, 115, 122, 130
Arafat, Yassir, 33
Assassins of Memory, 7

Barbie, Klause, 27, 28, 29
Baynac, Jacques, 90
Betar, 109, 111-114, 120-124
Biographical Companion to Modern Thought, 70

Carlos the Jackal, 29
Chmielnicki massacres, 19
Chomsky Reader, 71, 91
Chomsky, William Zev, 38
Chomsky's Preface, 58
Commentary, 4, 5
Communism with the Mask Off, 77

Council Communism, 99-103
Crossroads to Israel, 108

Daily Express, 49, 50
Deir Yassin, 126-130
Denying the Holocaust, 5
Dresden, 130

Éditions de la Différence, 64
Eisenmenger, Johann, 18

Fateful Triangle, 22, 32, 77, 106-132
Faurisson, Robert, 2, 5, 9-11, 21, 40, 42-64, 68-71, 75, 82, 83, 86, 87, 89, 97, 98, 102, 133
Finkielkraut, Alain, 101
Flapan, Simha, 109-111, 121-124
Flat Earth Research Society, 90

Index

Fresco, Nadine, 11, 49, 90

From Haven to Conquest, 109, 116

genocide, 8, 44
Genoud, Francois, 28
Guillaume, Pierre, 2, 22, 43, 53, 56-65, 71, 75, 87, 103, 104, 132
Gypsies, 5-7

Herman, Edward, 56
Holocaust, 2, 5, 6, 9, 20, 21, 31, 38, 45, 46, 48, 51, 54, 61, 62, 65, 69, 71, 74, 81, 83, 86, 87, 118, 130, 133
Hotel Terminus, 27, 29

Institute for Historical Review, 31, 32, 50, 77, 90
The International Jew, 31, 77
Irgun Tsvai Leumi, 127

Jabotinsky, Vladimir, 109, 110

Jewish History, Jewish Religion, 19
Journal of Historical Review, 65, 73

Keegstra, 51
Khalidi, Walid, 109, 116-119
Khissas, 127
Korsch, Karl, 98, 100

La Vieille Taupe, 52, 53, 56-58, 60, 61, 65-68, 99, 102
Laqueur, Walter, 4, 5
Lazare, Bernard, 66
Le Matin, 9
Le Monde, 40
Lemkin, Raphael, 8
Leninist League, 92, 94
Liberation, 9
Lies of Our Time, 32
Lilienthal, Alfred, 55, 77, 105
Lipstadt, Deborah, 5
Lokhamei Kherut Yisrael, 127
Lord Beaverbrook, 49
Luxemburg, Rosa, 99

Index

malign equivalence, 88, 90, 96
Manufacturing Consent, 32
Marlen, 89, 91-98, 99, 111
Marlenites, 91, 92-95, 98
Marx, Karl, 4, 24, 72, 91, 93, 95, 96
Marxism and the Bolshevik State, 95
Mattick, Paul, 98, 100, 103
Method of the Crucial Source, 47
Morris, Stephen, 42
Mufti of Jerusalem, 118, 119, 124-126
Mussolini, Benito, 24, 109, 121, 122

National Bolsheviks, 25
Necessary Illusions, 32
New Left, 27
New York Times, 13, 39, 40
Noontide Press, 31, 77

Ogmios, 43, 64, 67

Pacifica Radio, 32
Paris, Erna, 28
Peace in the Middle East, 86
Personal History, 115
Pirates and Emperors, 32
PLO, 33, 35
The Plot Against Christianity, 77
Political Economy of Human Rights, 56, 63
Porath, Y., 112, 113
Protocols of the Learned Elders of Zion, 31, 77

Rassinier, Paul, 64, 102
Réponses inédites, 63
revisionism, 45, 72
Rosenthal, A. M., 13-15, 21
Rubinstein, Bill, 63, 69, 70, 79, 87

Sampson, Geoffrey, 70, 71, 83, 84
Samson complex, 74, 131, 132
Schlesinger, Arthur, 4

Index

self-hatred, 3, 4, 89, 105

Shahak, Israel, 3, 4, 18, 19, 20, 34

Shaw Commission, 112, 115

Sheean, Vincent, 109, 111, 114-119

Shoah, 65

Sobran, Joseph, 10

Socialisme ou Barbarie, 101

Spartacus, 64

Spiro, George, 92-98

Stäglich, Wilhelm, 64, 103

Stein, Howard F., 73-75, 88, 105, 131, 132

Streicher, Julius, 105

Sykes, Christopher, 108, 110, 113, 114, 128

Thion, Serge, 53, 58, 64, 69, 72, 82, 83, 132, 133, 134

Third Position, 25

Towards a New Cold War, 4

Unhealed Wounds, 28

Vergès, Jacques, 27-30

Vidal, Gore, 19

Vidal-Naquet, Pierre, 7, 11, 101

Vieille Taupe, La, 25, 43, 44, 52, 64, 66-71, 91, 99, 101-103

Voltaire, 11, 12, 80

Vrba, Rudolf, 47

Weber, Mark, 56

Z Magazine, 32

The Zionist Connection, 77

Zundel, 51, 81